Shot In The Head

A Sister's Memoir, A Brother's Struggle

By

Katherine Flannery Dering

Dering, Katherine Flannery, 1947-, author
    Shot in the head : a sister's memoir a brother's struggle / by

Katherine Flannery Dering.
        ISBN 978-1-927637-21-0 (pbk.)

    1. Dering, Katherine Flannery, 1947-. 2. Flannery, Paul--

Mental health. 3. Schizophrenics--Family relationships--United

States. 4. Schizophrenics--United States--Biography. 5. Brothers

and sisters--United States. I. Title.

    RC514.D474 2014   616.89'80092   C2013-908586-6

First Published by Bridgeross in Dundas, ON, Canada

To all the orderlies and social workers and nursing assistants who care for our elderly and infirm with patience and respect, day after day after day.

Author's statement

Memory is a strange and insubstantial thing. My brother Paul suffered from multiple delusions, often anguished by memories of events that had never happened. I've done my best to accommodate the eight slightly different versions of the past held by my eight remaining siblings. In the end, though, it's my book, my version. The book's dialogue and the sequence of events, especially scenes from fifty years ago, are my best efforts to present what really took place. Any remaining inaccuracies (and there inevitably may be a few) would not alter the essence of the presentation of lives lived. A few names of non-family members have been changed to protect their privacy, but everything else is as it happened.

Advance Reviews

"Both universal and personal, Katherine Dering's Shot in the Head is the story of a family just barely holding on. Dering unspools her story with urgent compassion and grace."

Elizabeth Eslami, author of *Bone Worship and Hibernate* and the 2013 winner of the Ohio State University Prize in Short Fiction.

"During the past half century our treatment system for persons with serious mental illness has become a fragmented disaster. Katherine Dering's book is about her middle class family's odyssey during this time as it tries to ensure that her brother with schizophrenia receives adequate services. The book is an extremely well crafted, compelling drama about how a large group of caring siblings interact and cope as their brother becomes severely ill, is repeatedly hospitalized, and endures various attempts to "transition" him into the community. This eye-opening account of the realities of having a seriously mentally ill family member should be at the top of the "must read" list for anyone involved with, or otherwise interested in, improving mental health services for those who are most in need.

Fred Frese, Ph.D. Associate Professor of Psychiatry Northeast Ohio Medical University Coordinator, Recovery Project

"When mental illness happens, it affects the whole family. Much has been written about the effect on parents, but not enough about the grief - and importance - of siblings. You will fall in love with the Flannery clan, who stepped up to support their brother Paul throughout his sad journey with schizophrenia. This book takes you through the frustration, the loss, the mistakes and wishful thinking - and, ultimately the love and support that shines through it all - as the family struggles to understand the illness and the system, stay together, and also show Paul how much he is loved -

all while trying to focus on their own lives as well. This is a readable and important book that will open the reader's eyes to the effects of schizophrenia, the need for change, and the power of family love."

Randye Kaye, author, *Ben Behind His Voices: One Family's Journey from the Chaos of Schizophrenia to Hope*

"So powerful and emotional"

Ann Cloonan, Director, Bedford Free Library, Bedford, NY

1. Hawks on the River

It was mid-October and my turn to visit my brother Paul at his nursing home. His next oncologist's appointment wasn't for two weeks, and I didn't really know what to do with him. Over the past thirty years, it had been one visit every month or two, an awkward burger and fries at a diner and a quick look at a few pictures of the nieces and nephews before I dropped him back at his mental hospital or group home. With all the doctor visits lately, we'd already been through all that. I decided to take him for a little drive.

It was a beautiful fall day in the Hudson Valley, the maples and ashes all red and gold, the sun warm through the car windows. Chemo treatments were taking their toll; Paul's face looked pasty in the sunlight. He was quiet today. He stared out at the streetscape as we drove past the hospital and on down Main Street as if he were memorizing every house, every bodega.

Downtown Peekskill, NY is an old, working man's town, but the factories all shuttered years ago. Today, our drive took us past dollar stores, thrift shops, and some public housing, all dark brick and sterile cement walkways. We didn't see anyone walking on the sidewalks. We stopped at a dollar store and Paul bought a two-liter bottle of Pepsi, a little plastic pumpkin and a deck of cards.

Back in the car, we drove slowly toward the train tracks and the Hudson River. Facing the riverfront park where we sometimes fed the gulls stood a wall of hundred-year-old brick buildings. Once stove and gunpowder factories or ship merchants' offices, they were now delis and Irish pubs with peeling signs for happy hours and ladies' nights. We passed them, drove a couple of miles north on Route 9, along the eastern side of the river onto Route 202 and pulled off at a high look-out spot, a half-mile south of the Bear Mountain Bridge. Some conservationist group had put up signs describing how eagles made nests nearby. We got out of the car and stood against the low stone wall, leaning out into the breeze, breathing the crisp fall air and trying to catch a glimpse of one of the big birds soaring in the distance. One circled far overhead then disappeared.

Down below I could see how the Hudson River turned away to the west just south of us. On our side of the river and beneath our lookout, on the outside of the river's curve, the water had scoured out a stony cliff. Across from us, in the crook of the curve, the meandering river had left a large alluvial plain on which a tiny green tractor was sitting at the edge of a brown, stubbled field. It was low, boggy land, part tidal marsh and an estuarine sanctuary, winter home to bald eagles and any number of water fowl. As I gazed across at the field, letting the sun play

8

on my face, I imagined being the workman driving that tractor, the smell of newly turned earth filling my nostrils, the sound of the motor drowning out the steady whooshing noise of the river behind me. The workman would be totally unaware of Paul and me standing up on this bluff. He'd be oblivious to the river's curve, how it straightened for a ways just south of here, how it meandered past the other-worldly nuclear reactor at Indian Point, just around that next curve. He would only know this flat, fertile soil and nearby wildlife.

A barge made its way slowly upriver, heavy with cargo. Paul watched it. Then he blew on his hands and pulled his knit cap down over his ears and straggly-haired, chemo head.

"You're cold, aren't you?"

He nodded and hugged himself.

"Let's go get some coffee somewhere and warm up." We went back to the car.

"I just don't feel so good," he said, shaking his head slowly and holding his hands over the warm air vents. It was fifty degrees outside. I moved the heat to a higher setting and gave him the blue paisley lap robe I kept for him in the back. He leaned into his seat, the blanket pulled up to his chin, and closed his eyes. I fiddled with the radio.

"Do you believe in reincarnation?" he asked me, his eyes still closed.

Paul and I were raised Catholic. But it had been a long time since the Baltimore Catechism.

"I'm not sure," I said. Where was he going with this? "How about you?"

He sat up and nodded emphatically, pulling his chin up, till it nearly touched the tip of his nose. "I do," he said. "I do. It's better than clouds and harps." He laughed, then stopped to cough, coughed some more, and grabbed some tissues from the pack on the floor and spat into them. He balled them up and stuffed them into his pocket. "I got the shitty end of the stick this time," he said.

He paused and looked at me. "I didn't mind doing my turn for all of you, though. Don't get me wrong," he said – hands out, palms down, an umpire calling safe. "I mean, you guys have been the best."

We were driving along the edge of Bear Mountain, back down the winding road toward Peekskill and his nursing home.

"You did have an unlucky time this cycle," I said, trying to watch the road. "What would you want to come back as next time? How about as an eagle?"

He didn't need time to think.

"Naw," he said. "Next time I just want to be one of the sane ones." He chuckled softly and looked out the window.

On the other side of the low guardrail, the hillside dropped away almost straight down to the river, far below. The eagles were nowhere to be seen.

2. Shot

"I was shot in the head," Paul told the daughter of his 80 year-old roommate one day. "Some mugger. I've been all screwed up ever since."

"I just heard about your brother," she said when I arrived at the nursing home later that day. She was a sincere woman, eyebrows creased in a look of perpetual worry. She brushed a shock of thick black hair off her forehead with the back of her hand and then reached to grasp mine. "How awful! They never caught the mugger?"

How to say it? Mugged, shot, scalped…

Paul was scalped when he was 16. His brains escaped with his blood and skin in scarlet rivers, oozing from his skull and down his pale neck, past the football shoulders, past his chest and back and groin, between the webbed toes that were just like Grandpa's, and sank into the dry pine floor of his third-floor bedroom in our old house in White Plains.

In actuality a toothless 48-year old with schizophrenia, Paul needed nebulizer treatments twice a day for his bad lungs. Chronic pulmonary something or other, a doctor said. He also suffered from anosognosia; like many mentally ill people, he didn't really believe he was mentally ill. He *must* have been mugged, shot, beaten, scalped, head bashed playing football or concussed from a ski fall. *Some*thing must have made him this way.

At Hedgewood, the adult home where he used to be warehoused, his cough and fever had received only desultory medical attention. In the daily din of fights, breakdowns and police squad cars, the staff hardly noticed he was ill. When he was too sick to get out of bed, overworked attendants there sent

11

him to the local hospital, where medical personnel mumbled about pneumonia and possible TB.

Months later, at Westledge Nursing Facility, the resident doctor reviewed all his charts. "What's this unexplained mass in this man's lung?" he asked. No one knew. He suggested a biopsy.

"They'll need to insert a probe into your lung," he said. "But it won't hurt; we'll use anesthesia."

"NO!" Paul said. "No operations. I know what you're doing. You're going to take out my lungs. I'll die."

Many phone calls and visits later, my sister Monica and I finally convinced him this was not a plot to steal his lungs. Monica was two years older than Paul; she was seventh of the Flannery brood, born when our parents were approaching 40 and already exhausted. "I'm having my kids when I'm young enough to play with them," she announced to Mother one day when she was about ten. And she did just that. Her children grown, a respiratory therapist now, Monica went to the test with Paul to explain what was going on.

Ilene, Paul's twin, went also, to hold his hand. The twins were eighth and ninth of the ten children. Petite and demure as a young child, a little dark-eyed doll, Ilene was now tall and outgoing, with long, straight dark hair and hooded hazel eyes. She never pulled back from Paul, no matter how distressing his behavior. She treated her twin's mental illness as if it were a broken ankle or ruptured appendix, some sort of medical anomaly that needed to be fixed.

From: Ilene Wells
To: Sheila Flannery, Katherine Dering, Charlotte Flannery, Grace Flannery, Laurie Flannery, Patrick Flannery, Monica Leggett, Julia Brower, Loretta Pontillo, Charlotte Pontillo, Melissa Leggett, Shelly Flannery, Sean

---

Flannery, Kerry Flannery, John Flannery, Russell Leggett, Meghan Mahoney, Lucy Lesperance, more...
Date: July 27, 2007 1:25 PM
Subject: Paul

I just got a call from the pulmonologist who did the biopsy. Paul has "non-small cell" lung cancer. No results yet on the lymph nodes. That will be in the next day or two. Non-small cell vs. small cell doesn't make a difference as far as how bad it is, apparently. It just tells them what type of treatment plans they need to do.

We made an appointment with Dr. Ayan, an oncologist, and the pulmonologist is contacting the hospital to get the results sent to him. He said he'd call him as well. He indicated that the cancer has only been here for maybe 3 - 4 months - not when Paul first went in for pneumonia a couple of years ago. So, that tells me that if St. Joe's had run tests when he went in a couple of months ago - when they first detected the mass - we could have had a two month jump on this. If it's grown that big in 3 - 4 months, then a two month jump really means a lot!

Dr. Ayan wants to have a PET scan done. It will show how far it has spread, if it has spread.

Katherine, would you work with West Ledge to get him over there this week if Dr. Ayan wants to try to get the scan done before the appt. on Friday? I will be heading out to Hyannis soon, and will be back Thursday night.

Let's hope we get some better news from the results on the lymph node and the PET scan. I just hope we can do some sort of treatment that isn't too harsh and that will give him some quality of life for a few years anyway.
Ilene

A few days later Monica and I picked up Paul to get the results of the PET scan. The usual round of smiling hellos from the nursing staff. A few elderly residents sat wordless in wheelchairs at the door to their rooms while attendants changed their sheets or washed the floor. Paul was pacing in his room. Monica used her mother voice with him. "Now go to the bathroom before we leave. Where's your water bottle? You're dehydrated." As children, Paul and Monica were fair and blue-eyed. They both took after Dad and our mostly Irish ancestors.

Monica, Paul and I met up with Ilene outside the oncologist's office. With our straight dark hair and darker eyes, Ilene and I took more after Mother and the French-Canadian side of the family.

When Ilene greeted Paul she leaned into him, wrapping an arm around his shoulders then smoothing his hair as they walked. It was a warm day, sunny, a pleasant breeze. Dwarf fruit trees lined the walkway to the doctor's offices sending a sweet scent into the air. Little birds chirped and rustled through the branches. A walk in the park. Surely this would be a very early stage cancer, something easily treated.

The air conditioning was cranked up in the waiting room and it was cold. Paul seemed nervous, getting up to check himself in the rest room mirror every few minutes. Making sure his hair was still there, that his eyes and nose were where they should be. But who wouldn't be nervous?

Ilene said she thought he was making much more sense lately. Maybe he was maturing out of the worst of the delusions. Doctors had said he might. As testosterone levels wane, men with mental illness sometimes see a lessening of psychotic symptoms.

"Mr. Flannery?" the receptionist called.

We made Paul take the seat nearest to the doctor's desk. The three of us sat in a row behind him.

After a few hellos, the doctor, a slightly built man from Pakistan, put his head down and read through Paul's charts. Lanky, restless, Paul clenched and released his jaws and stirred the air with his knees. Suddenly he doubled over in a coughing fit. He coughed and choked, gasped a bit, spat a wad of phlegm into some tissues, then leaned back in his chair, breathing slowly and noisily through his nose. A hissing radiator.

He'd been like this for months.

The doctor looked up. "Well, Mr. Flannery," he began, "I'm sorry to tell you, but you definitely have lung cancer."

In an instant, Paul leaped up, reached across the desk and grabbed at the doctor's collar.

Ilene jumped and dragged him away by his shoulders. "Paul, no!"

The doctor pulled back and pressed himself against the crammed bookcase behind him. His eyes were wide. Paul was six feet tall and still strong, despite having lost 30 or 40 pounds in the past few months.

"I don't have cancer. You're just making it up to take my money," Paul shouted, shaking off Ilene and waving his fist.
His world was filled with dangerous people. They could steal his innermost thoughts with a simple stare. He sometimes stared back, usually adding a growling noise and a lip curl, sending people fleeing from diners and dollar stores.

"He's no problem," I said. "He won't hurt you. He's just upset."

Both hands on Paul's shoulders, Ilene made soothing noises and urged him into his chair. "Let's just hear what he has to say, OK?"

The doctor adjusted his collar and remained huddled against the bookcase, a bit back from the desk, a small, pressed-wood affair. It was a cramped office with mismatched chairs and struggling houseplants on the window ledge. The patients we had seen in the waiting room were largely elderly people or indigents, like Paul. Medicaid payments were not generous.

The doctor's dark eyes scanned the three of us like a startled deer.

Ilene rubbed Paul's back in big circles. "He's trying to help you," she said.

15

"It was just some acne. I had some really bad acne that slid down into my lungs," Paul said. He waved his arms and shifted his weight back and forth in the small space. Ilene hung on him. "It's all just puss. I've coughed it all out now, though. I coughed and I coughed." He shook his head, remembering the effort. "So I know it is definitely, positively, *not* cancer."

The coughing had not healed his schizophrenia, obviously.

Ilene pulled Paul back to his chair, where his legs resumed their scissoring.

The doctor went back to his desk. He explained that Paul was in stage three, of four stages, with four being the worst. His cancer was inoperable, as it was in three different spots in the lungs and two different lymph nodes. With chemo, though, his chances of recovery were 50-50. Monica jotted pertinent details down in a notebook and asked Paul, "Did you understand that, Paul? Do you want to ask him anything?" Paul curled one lip like an angry Elvis and shook his head no.

"What do we do next?" Monica asked.

Ilene held Paul's hand with one of hers and stroked it with her other.

I hardly heard what the doctor was saying. I looked at Paul, his mouth puckering and loosening, masticating invisible gum. There was a buzzing in my ears. I saw Paul in my arms, crying as the holy water dripped onto his head at his baptism; Paul at three or four, sliding in his socks, falling and whacking his head on the wood floor in the dining room; an adult Paul gobbling a burger, slobbering ketchup and meat juice all down his face and shirt. I heard my daughters and nieces complaining to me that he ruined every family get-together. "Does Uncle Paul have to be there?"

Did we even want him to get better? I immediately felt guilty for even thinking it. The diagnosis was not unexpected, but I felt unprepared. What should my role be in all this? My

16

hands lay open in my lap, and I tried to focus.

The doctor was talking about what would be involved in treatments: chemo and radiation, mostly. Paul would experience nausea, the radiation would burn. There would be blood tests and doctor visits and lengthy sessions in hospitals; a long haul, with no guarantees.

"What do you think, Kathy? Should I do it?" Paul asked.

Paul, Ilene and Monica all looked at me. Of the four siblings present, I was the oldest in the room. I looked at those pale blue eyes pleading with me, the unkempt hair, the frayed, too-large sweatshirt. I thought about the delusions and breakdowns and the foul adult home he would probably go back to if he made it through.

"Do you want to live?" I asked.

"I want to live. Absolutely." Paul nodded his head up and down. If he had any teeth, he would have gritted them.

"Well, the doctor says you have a chance. I'd do it."

The doctor's brows furrowed and his mouth turned down at the corners. "This will require a great deal of patient cooperation," he warned, shaking his head as he spoke. "There will be many, many procedures. I see that he has not always cooperated in the past. He'll have to comply with blood tests and the other regimens or it won't work."

"He'll cooperate," Ilene chimed in. "Won't you Paul?"

Paul was squinting at the doctor and growling.

The doctor ran his finger between his collar and his neck again. "And I have the nurses to think of," he said. "I'll have to insist that one of you accompany him every time." He made eye contact with Ilene, then Monica, then me. It felt like he lingered with me.

Ilene had a travel job and was often out of town from Monday through Friday. Most of our other siblings either worked full time or lived too far away to do much. Over the past twenty-five years, I'd often worked stressful, 60-hour weeks

17

in my role as chief financial officer (CFO) of a community bank. Our oldest sister, Sheila, had been the primary contact for him for years until Ilene stepped up a year ago. These days I seldom saw him more than once every two or three months. Monica, with younger children and living further away from Paul's various hospitals and group homes, had seen even less of him.

I've done enough, I wanted to say. Second of the ten children, I'd had enough of cleaning up after little siblings. Enough feedings and bottles and diapers and bath times and tending to cuts and bruises. But "family first," as Mother always used to say. She had dropped everything to help me look after my two girls when I got divorced many years before. I took a deep breath and felt my body shift into a resigned position. Like Monica, I was working only part time now. We looked at each other. Somehow, we'd share the burden. We'd figure it out.

3. Childhood by Numbers

I was second of the eventual ten Flannery kids, Paul eighth. The home we all lived in from my third to sixth grades – before Paul was born – was a comfortable brick, Tudor-style house in an entire neighborhood of red brick houses in neat rows in Grosse Pointe Park, a modest suburb of Detroit.

John and Katherine about 1953

There were crocheted afghans draped on comfy couches in dens and tuna noodle casserole on Fridays. We were a family of Mass on Sunday and grace before meals, guardian angels, incense and holy cards of saints with golden halos. There were hula hoop contests in the parking lot of St. Clare of Montefalco School and dancing lessons taught by Miss Pat in the black and white linoleum-tiled school basement.

My older sister Sheila and I rode our bikes to the park and the library, coming home with baskets full of books by Enid Blyton and C. S. Lewis. My friend Katie and I played with our Ginny dolls. My brother Johnny and I climbed trees and hid out on garage roofs. From the tall pine tree in Harry Chrysler's back yard, you could see all the way to Lake St. Clair, where freighters went by, hauling taconite and other freight to and from Duluth and the factories in Detroit, Cleveland and Buffalo.

With a new baby sibling every year or two, our house

19

was pretty crowded. But Sheila and I had the third floor all to ourselves. We even had our own bathroom. The previous occupants had left us blue wall-to-wall carpeting and pirate-themed wallpaper. Some of the pirates, nearly as large as their ships, floated mysteriously against the azure sky. They sneered defiantly at us, brandishing curved scabbards and smoking muskets. The teleplay of Peter Pan had been shown on TV a few months after we moved in, in 1955, and the wallpaper pirates soon became Peter's enemies.

Crocodiles lurked under my bed. Picture books strewn strategically across the blue carpet ocean became my path to the bathroom. I became expert at imaginary sword-fighting. I'd leap from my bed brandishing a ruler-sword, tiptoe across my literary archipelago and walk carefully back and forth along the bathtub edge, practicing to walk the plank. I became fixated on flying off to Never Never Land with Peter – not as Wendy, with all her motherly ways, but as one of the lost boys, or perhaps an Indian princess. I'd had enough of mothering, helping with my many little siblings. I wanted adventures with Indians and pirates and no one ever really getting hurt. I left my window open a crack for Peter for years, much to my father's annoyance. "Who left this window open again? Geez! Do you think we should heat all of Detroit this winter?"

Mother was always busy with the latest babies. Charlotte and Monica (sixth and seventh) were born while we lived in this house. Mother was a stern woman, very efficient, a child on the hip, a cigarette burning in the ashtray, some household chore always underway. Never "mom" or "mommy," and decidedly never "ma," Mother was field marshal commandant of the children's forces and Sheila and I were often conscripted into service. After school there were mounds of diapers to fold, clean clothes to put away in little ones' rooms, dishes to wash or a baby to jiggle or change.

Dad was seldom home. For many years, he attended law

school four nights a week, in addition to working all day. Weekends, he studied or watched Tigers baseball or the Detroit Red Wings, depending on the season. He already had an MBA from Stanford University, but he never did practice law. He had planned to go into labor relations with the JD degree, but somehow, with four, five, six children, it never seemed a good time to shift careers.

Above all the hubbub, Sheila and I lived in our own little world. Most of the time, that meant parents and little kids did not ascend the third floor staircase. We could have a Monopoly game going for days, and no babies would mess up the board. We hated turning off the lights at night (crocodiles and pirates, see above). As a compromise, we got to keep the bathroom light on and leave the door ajar just a crack, allowing a thin shaft of light to pierce the shadows. Unfortunately, the light also hit against the wallpaper and lit up the pirates' eyeballs, which glared out, menacingly. I kept my Jesus, Blessed Virgin and Holy Family fluorescent glow-in-the-dark statues directly next to the light bulb of our bed-side lamp for several minutes before lights went out. Once darkness fell and the eyeballs glistened, my glowing Catholic talismans were there to defend me.

We were comfortable there in Grosse Pointe. There were long summer days on the shores of Lake St. Clair, fireworks at the park on the 4th of July and cold walks in winters to our classrooms at St. Clare School. We had tons of friends, twenty first cousins, a full complement of grandparents, aunts, uncles, second cousins once removed, first cousins thrice removed, great aunts and uncles on farms in Indiana and Ontario, and a steady future just waiting for us to grow into.

Dad was a car company executive who was going places.

***

There were seven children when Dad's job with Chrysler moved us to Switzerland, where Paul and Ilene were born. Our flight to Europe was first class all the way, including roomy

21

seats, attentive stewards and stewardesses, and pull-down berths like those in a train's Pullman car. A crowd of Dad's business associates met us at the Geneva airport and escorted us downtown to the luxurious Hotel Richemond, where we lived for the six weeks until our furniture arrived.

I was just starting seventh grade, and I'd never been in a restaurant before, much less a hotel. My biggest trip had been to visit Great Aunt Loretta on her farm in Kokomo, Indiana – about a five or six hour drive from our home. But now we were met at every turn by doormen who bowed and bobbed in maroon uniforms with brass buttons and smart, braided hats. We shared four connected bedrooms and a sitting room, with green silk jacquard draperies over French doors that led out to small balconies with wrought iron railings. Maids wore neat maroon dresses with little white aprons and curtsied. And each room had its own bathroom – with a bidet. There was a lot of giggling over that fixture! Johnny and I liked to order bacon and toast to our own rooms, and any time, day or night they would bring us mounds of it, (until the room service bill arrived and we were cut off.)

In front of the hotel was a formal, manicured park with a small gazebo and meticulously maintained beds of golden marigolds, red geraniums and rainbow-hued petunias. To the right, we could look up the Rue du Mont Blanc to the imposing Geneva train station and the Jura mountains behind it. Looking down the street to the left, toward Lake Geneva, we could see the *jet d'eau*– a huge, single jet of water which rose 200 feet above the city and was its symbol. And beyond the *jet d'eau*, far to the south, loomed the spectacular, snow-covered Mont Blanc. I liked to go downstairs alone and find a little table on the hotel's terrace across from the park and order breakfast. Positioned so I could see Mont Blanc, I'd eat my crusty, freshly-baked *petit pains* with sweet butter and strawberry jam and just revel in it all.

The whole family ate at a different, first-class restaurant

22

nearly every night. Tuxedoed waiters often greeted the parade of children invading their posh eateries with pursed lips, their noses firmly in the air. But we didn't care. At some point during the first week of our stay we discovered *flambé*. Imagine! We could have waiters stand by our table and set our food on fire! Steak Diane and cherries jubilee became our favorites. What fun! (again, until we were cut off.) Monica, only two years old, used to fall asleep with her face in her plate almost every night. It got to be a contest who could spot her as she wobbled and warn Mother so she could shield her face from too hard or messy a landing.

Eventually the furniture arrived and the hotel life ended. Our rented house was in a new development just outside Geneva near several small farms in the old village of Genthod. We found little to see or even hear there, beyond wheat and corn fields and the murmuring noises of cattle and sheep on quiet evenings. We had no TV, and our French was still too poor to be able to enjoy the books at the local library; school wouldn't start for weeks. Cut off from any friends or TV, my brothers and sisters and I sang songs and climbed trees, played in the neighboring wheat and corn fields, or wandered through a stretch of woods a mile or so away, where we liked to bounce and sing cowboy songs on a favorite, fallen tree trunk that hung over a small stream.

Mother and Dad took the oldest five to Rome and we toured the Vatican, leaving Monica and Charlotte with our new au-pair, Elizabeth, a 17-year old Swiss-German girl from a small village near Zurich. We climbed to the top of the Leaning Tower of Pisa and the dome of St. Peter's. We saw the Pope.

Mother was expecting the twins, although we did not yet know it was twins, and as the pregnancy progressed, she was often forced to nap, or at least sit with her feet up. But we kept ourselves occupied. One rainy day we discovered the old record player, for which Dad had finally gotten a transformer to run on

Europe's 220-volt electricity. There weren't many records–
mostly a few Broadway show albums and some old, single-sided
78's acquired when we broke up Great Aunt Mary's apartment
to put her in a nursing home a year or two before.

Of the more modern records, the soundtrack from the
movie version of *High Society* was our favorite. Mother and Dad
had bought it after seeing the movie musical a year or two
before. We played it over and over again and soon memorized
every word. We had no idea what the movie was about, but we
pored over the pictures on the record jacket of Grace Kelly, Bing
Crosby, Frank Sinatra, Celeste Holme, and Louis Armstrong, his
eyes bulging and the ubiquitous white handkerchief held in the
hand with the horn.

"Who wants to be a millionaire?" Frank Sinatra sang.

Celeste Holme answered, mockingly, "I don't!"

"Have fancy houses everywhere?"

"I don't!" she answered again. Johnny and I always
shouted out "I DO!" and screamed with delight.

1960. Clockwise around the piano, Mary Grace, Mother, Charlotte, Pat,
Ilene, Paul and Johnny. Behind them Monica, Dad, Katherine and Sheila.

We loved to listen to Louis Armstrong singing in his gravelly voice,

"To see the scenery floating by...
We're now approaching Newport, Rhode "I"
In high, high so-,
High soci-
High society."

We tried hopelessly to make our young voices do that throat scraping, Satchmo thing.

Sometimes we pinched ourselves; we couldn't believe our good luck.

In the fall we attended the *Ecole Internationale* in downtown Geneva. Unlike our school in Michigan, there were no nuns or uniforms, and our classmates were Pakistani, American, British, German, African, and Israeli. Many of them, offspring of NATO or World Health Organization employees or children of movie stars, had moved from country to country before. The son of Yul Brynner! The daughter of Rita Hayworth! The boarding students were a rarefied lot.

The school was some distance from our home. Chrysler operated a school bus that ran through the suburbs picking up the younger kids, and Sheila and I could hitch a ride with them in the morning. But the junior and senior highs let out an hour later than the elementary school. Sheila and I became experienced commuters, taking two different trams to the Geneva train station, a commuter train to Genthod, and a long walk to get home from school every day.

Autumn passed quickly. We made scads of new friends. Mother went into labor while Dad was in South Africa on one of his many business trips, and he rushed back to the news that this delivery would be twins. With the assistance of complete bed rest, the babies held on for another three weeks and were born Christmas Day.

Paul, Ilene, summer 1960

How auspicious! Paul was so beautiful, with his blond curls and long, lanky body! Even his fingers were long and elegant. Ilene, two pounds smaller than Paul, was tiny and had straight dark hair and intense dark eyes set into a little round face. She looked like the Japanese dolls friends had sent us from Occupied Japan a few years before.

With Mother on bed rest, Dad did the Christmas shopping that year and the five oldest all got new, English-style racing bikes with three speeds and hand brakes as our big gifts, quite a change from our beat-up old Schwinns. The twins were baptized a few weeks later in the tiny, Medieval stone church in the nearby town of Versoix, each dressed in a piece of the Christening gown my father and the older seven children had been baptized in. Sheila and I held them for the service, filling in for the official godparents, who were back in the States.

Our au pair, Elizabeth, took on a lot of responsibility for Mother at this time, but there was still plenty of work for Sheila and me. When it was time for the twins to be fed, I was often called into service. Mother would sit them in their twin stroller on the black and white marble tile hallway next to the kitchen, and I'd sit opposite them and dip the baby spoon into the dish of rice cereal or applesauce or mashed potatoes and egg and feed first one, then the other. Little birds. Ilene was so petite, I'd urge her to open her tiny mouth and still the baby spoon barely fit. Paul would open his mouth wide enough for a freight train to run through! The slender spoon looked silly in that wide open expanse.

In the meantime, I came into adolescence with a vengeance. The American and British high school set got together on weekends at parties in the basement of the American Church, where we danced to Neil Sedaka, the Everly Brothers and the Brothers Four. I slow danced with my first boyfriend, Tommy Briton, who was a blond boy from Seattle. He kissed me on the mouth and for Christmas gave me a charm bracelet with the flags of all the Swiss cantons. I still have it.

In March we went on a five-day ski vacation in the Jura Mountains. Mother and Dad stayed at friends' ski chalet, ate fondue, and sat around a metal-hooded, freestanding fireplace drinking kirsch and looking incredibly chic. James Bond had nothing on this crowd! We kids stayed at a children's *pension*, where our rooms were heated, and we ate hearty, simple meals and went to bed early. We all took ski lessons. I fell the third day doing a snowplow on an icy patch. My knee swelled up to the size of a honeydew melon, and I enjoyed a great deal of sympathy as I sat by the fire for the duration of our stay.

The next August we returned to Detroit for our one-month home leave in triumph! Hail conquering heroes! Jack Kennedy was running for President. All our relatives were excited. This was to be a new world. A Catholic in the White House! Mother had her hair done in a bouffant and wore pillbox hats. Watching Bobby Kennedy's big family in the news, we felt proud to be a big, Irish Catholic family. Dad always used to say, "There are winners and losers in this world." We were among the winners. Everyone said Mother looked just like

27

Jackie.

On our way back to Geneva after home leave, we stopped off for a week in Portugal, where we rented a small bus and driver. He ferried us back and forth from the beaches to our resort hotel in the mountains outside of Estoril and took us to see the shrine to Our Lady at Fatima. We were riding high. Nursemaids, deluxe hotels, everything first class.

We suffered a blow that December: Grandpa Flannery died suddenly of a brain hemorrhage the day after Christmas. Mother made us all kneel in a circle and say a rosary for his soul while Dad, an only child, made arrangements to fly home to Detroit and help his mother with the funeral. The living room floor was marble, the rug thin, and my knees hurt unbearably by the time we had finished the last Hail Mary and Glory Be. Then, in March, not quite two years after our trek had begun, Chrysler laid off almost all the men it had sent overseas and replaced them with lower-paid Swiss nationals. Thirty families were given three months' severance and passage back to Detroit. And just like that, the world as we knew it came to an end. Dad had lost his father and his job in three months, and he was never the same. Neither were we.

Mother planned a defiant grand tour for our return trip home. Towing along our new au pair, Marie Cecile, we drove down to Venice, where we took gondola rides and walked the twins up and down endless bridges over canals before boarding the Italian ocean liner *Vulcania* for a cruise around the Mediterranean, with stops in Greece, Sicily and Naples.

When we sailed into New York harbor ten days later, we were two parents, nine children and one au pair. We carried thirty-one suitcases and a big straw basket that Mother bought in Palermo, which now, in turn, carried Paul and Ilene's dirty diapers. There was no one to greet us when we disembarked. We kids sat for hours on the cobblestones under the old elevated

28

West Side Highway while Mother, Dad and Marie Cecile wrestled the luggage through customs. Finally, after two long days mostly on the Pennsylvania Turnpike, stuffed into our gold '57 Plymouth wagon and the white '59 Fiat 600 for the drive, the family arrived back in Detroit, where we split up and moved in with various relatives.

We were ruined; we felt it every time we looked at our parents.

It took Dad six months to find another job. The term "corporate downsizing" hadn't been invented back in 1961; as far as most employers were concerned, Dad had been fired. During those long months at Grandma's house in Detroit, Sheila and I helped fold and insert hundreds of letters and resumes into hundreds of envelopes for the big job search. There would be occasional moments of hope. This one may be it! Dad would be off for an interview in Cincinnati or Pittsburgh. Maybe we'd be moving to Virginia, maybe Belgium! But nothing panned out. And as we ate through all our savings and borrowed money from relatives, Dad fell into a deep depression.

Once a man on the way up, an international marketing maven, in his own mind at least, he spent months searching for another job before settling on one that paid half his former salary, in New York City, half a continent away from our family and friends in Detroit. While a professional job with a large corporation (Socony Mobil), his new position was as a senior financial analyst, several steps down from his previous managerial title and responsibilities.

When we piled back into the two cars for the two day drive back East, unbeknownst to us, Dad now carried a huge chip on his shoulder, although it was invisible at the time. Feeling betrayed, broken, hopeless, he would trudge through his remaining work years like an automaton.

Also invisible were the little schizophrenia molecules, mutated DNA, their pitchforks and cloven hoofs waiting patiently inside toddler Paul's head.

4. White Plains, New York

Painting of our house in White Plains by
M. Grace Flannery

1961. It was the height of the Cold War. When we settled into our new home in White Plains – a wood frame, green-shingled Victorian – Dad told us that an FBI spy named Philbrick, who had been made famous in a book and fifties TV show called "I Led Three Lives," had lived in our house some years before we moved in.

The place had been built in 1903 and boasted eight bedrooms, four bathrooms, a huge kitchen, miles of rotting gutters and walls full of decrepit plumbing that sprouted leaks at the least provocation. The huge, wrap-around porch was shrouded in overgrown evergreens that allowed little light into the downstairs rooms. The bedrooms were all covered in yellowed, peeling wallpaper, the stairs creaked, and the doorbell was incongruously magnificent, chiming like Big Ben.

We kids determined that if a spy had lived in our house, there had to be a secret room. Philbrick would have sat there in the middle of the night, tapping out Morse code messages to his FBI contacts, we were sure of it. In the restless days before we made new friends, we went around the second and third floors rapping on bedroom walls in our best Nancy Drew and Hardy Boys fashion, looking for hidden doors and loose panels. No luck.

An enormous laundry chute ran from the main second floor bathroom, down past the kitchen, where there was a convenient side door for tossing in dirty dish rags, and on to the basement laundry, where it let out into a wooden bin the size of a grown man. While the upstairs bathroom was a glamorous blue and white tile and chrome extravaganza, the laundry was a gloomy old place. Little light passed through its grimy, tiny windows, and its walls were covered in the original dark, bead-board paneling. The modern white washer and drier pair looked slightly out of place next to a cast iron, pot-belly stove, where we guessed the maids in the house's more prosperous years made fires to heat wash water and pressing irons.

One of us decided that the laundry chute must lead to the hidden room. (No one will now accept responsibility for this decision, but there it was.) We took turns kneeling and peering down the chute, shining the flashlight against the walls as far as we could see. But there was nothing *to* see. No tell-tale rectangular outline indicating some secret door or passageway.

Johnny and I figured we would have to explore the chute from the inside. He took Mother's clothesline and tied it to the pedestal of the bathroom sink and let it drop down the dark passage. We thought we might try repelling down the chute on the rope, but neither of us wanted to jump. I came up with the idea to try it from below. Flashlight in hand, I climbed into the

32

basement laundry bin, struggling over dirty underwear and baby clothes smelling of mashed peas and sour milk, found the rope and began pulling myself upward, all the while tapping on the sides, looking for the elusive entrance to Philbrick's hiding place. I was a pretty skinny fourteen year old, but it was a tight squeeze.

Tap, tap. Rat a tat.

"What do you see?" Johnny kept shouting down from the second floor bathroom.

I looked up as best I could, but I couldn't see him. I couldn't see anything except the metal walls of the chute, uniformly smooth, no rectangular outlines in sight.

Somewhere as I neared the kitchen, though, in the spot where clothes mysteriously got stuck from time to time, I saw that the chute turned 30 or 40 degrees. So that's why no light came down from above and I couldn't see Johnny! And then, my arms reaching upward, the walls of the chute pressing against my rib cage, I realized that I was wedged in. There was no way for me to go up or down. I panicked.

"I'm stuck, I'm stuck!"

"Hold on." Johnny called back.

He ran down to the basement, climbed into the smelly laundry bin and pulled on my legs till I broke free and landed on him in a squealing heap. And that was the end of our quest for the secret room. Except that we forgot to put away the rope, and in the wood molding around the chute door in the bathroom, the rope had worn a small groove.

Mother had worried since the day we moved in that Paul or Ilene might fall down the chute one day, so she checked it often. After our adventure, she noted the groove in the molding almost right away. But worse than the groove, she saw that we'd left the door open, a mortal sin in Flannery dogma. As punishment Johnny and I had to kneel on the bare wood floor in the dining room for two hours after dinner.

Back to reality.

Julia, our youngest, was born while I was a sophomore at White Plains High School, about a year after we moved in. Mother barely made it through that pregnancy; she was sick for most of Julia's first year on this earth with kidney infections and phlebitis. Both grandmothers came from Detroit and lived with us for months. There were diapers to fold, dishes, vacuuming, laundry, babies to bathe... we older girls had plenty of chores. Sheila hid in her room and read whenever possible. I joined as many clubs at school as I could – marching corps, synchronized swimming, Spanish club – but couldn't avoid most of it.

Money was tight now, every day a test to endure, our crowded home one bit of drudgery after another. Gone were the ski vacations in the Alps and summer excursions to Italy and Portugal. Now, if I needed new snow boots, I had to pay for them out of my babysitting money. No more au pair either; Marie Cecile went back to France a few months after we moved in. When a leg broke on the living room couch, it was propped up on a stack of books until Johnny and Pat found a better couch in the trash one night. Mother spent hours on her red metal stool at a counter in the telephone alcove off the kitchen, black coffee and Pall Malls at hand, juggling how to pay doctors or dentists or plumbers and still save enough for the A & P.

The middle kids all were enrolled at St. Bernard's parish school, which had only one classroom per grade. When it came time for Paul and Ilene to go to school, they became the first in our family to attend public elementary school, which had two classes per grade and so allowed the twins to be in separate classrooms. Mother thought that was important. It was also free. The older kids transferred over, as well. Most of the neighbors' kids went to the public school, anyway.

And our neighborhood had *plenty* of kids.

Ours was one of several rambling old houses full of huge Irish-Catholic families. There was a McGovern, Murphy,

34

McCullough, O'Reilly and/or a Flannery in almost every grade. The smaller, neater houses near us were generally home to Italian, Jewish or Protestant families and their 2.3 children. Our six sprawling blocks were crawling with kids who all ran in and out of each other's houses. It seemed there was often another little face at our already crowded dinner table. "You all have my blanket permission to accept any dinner invitation," Mother said. "Any time." And she meant it. There were neighborhood block parties and First Communions and Bar Mitzvahs. The little kids and twenty or thirty of their friends, my babysitting clients, lined the curbs and applauded when I left with my date to my first prom. "Ooh, Katherine. You look so pretty!" Like the Oscars.

Paul, Ilene and Julia hardly played a part in my life back them. They were just "little kids." They were part of the scenery, not part of my emotional life. The young ones had different trees to climb from the ones Johnny and I had climbed back in Michigan. Grandma Flannery nearly had a heart attack one day when she spotted Charlotte and Monica hanging by their knees from a top branch of a huge balsam fir by the back door. You could see all the way to the Long Island Sound from up on the top branches. This was their tree, like the trees in Grosse Pointe had been for Johnny and me.

In the lexicon of the older kids, "back in Geneva" became shorthand for "back when life was good." Here and now, life was bad. Johnny was hit by a car and nearly died of spinal meningitis. Mother nearly died after giving birth to Julia. Dad got grouchier and grouchier. Friends went skiing upstate, but I couldn't afford the lift ticket. I couldn't afford records, nylons, nice clothes, anything. If I wanted to hear the latest Motown 45's or Beatles' albums, I listened to them at a friend's house. I didn't even have a stereo to play them on. From a family scaling the heights, we had become a family trapped in some dark basement. To Paul, Ilene and Julia, this was the only home they knew; for me, it was just a place where we lived while I was in high school.

Before Dad got fired, I had been someone who always made instant best friends everywhere I went. But now I couldn't seem to connect. I depended on school clubs for the appearance of belonging. I went through all the motions of a typical suburban high school girl. I got my B+ grades and stayed out of trouble. But mostly, I just wanted to turn back the clock to return to Switzerland, where it seemed nothing was impossible. With one foot still in Switzerland and the other looking for a toehold someplace-anyplace else, I was a transient. My eyes were fixed on where I might go next, paying little attention to the drama unfolding at home.

For high school graduation, Sheila and I each got luggage, hers bright red and mine light blue. She hung around after graduation and, after a disastrous year at a nearby all girls' Catholic college, moved on to the local community college. But I got the message and left for a small Jesuit college upstate. Johnny and Mary Grace skedaddled in turn with their own graduation luggage. Patrick took off for Montana when he was 16. He stuffed jeans and tee shirts into one of Dad's old army duffel bags, slung his guitar case over his shoulder and stuck out his thumb. He formed a country rock band, toured the Northwest and Alaska, and we didn't hear from him for a decade.

At 13, with the oldest five away, Charlotte, number six, decided she would no longer be a middle child and declared herself the oldest of the little kids. The younger five, Paul smack in the middle, were growing up in a house that was always a little emptier, always a little quieter than the year before, with older siblings disappearing and no relatives for hundreds of miles. Unlike my first twelve years of plenty, theirs was a world of crumbling water pipes and cars that wouldn't start.

The five youngest, l to r Charlotte, Monica, Paul, Ilene, Julia,
Christmas 1966

The younger five – I refer to them to this day as the little kids – lived in an archeological dig, closets and dressers half full of departed older sisters' cast-off prom dresses, out-of-style skirts and sweaters and broken lipsticks and eyebrow pencils. Johnny and Patrick left Paul a closet with shelves of glass jars filled with dead beetles, discolored toe nails and dried up bird embryos. The third-floor wallpaper and ceiling bore stains of psychedelic paint, visible only by black light, as well as lines and lines of chemistry and physics equations and odd splotches from chemistry experiments gone awry. No more Pat Boone and no more Everly Brothers. At holidays, the little kids got to experience the Rolling Stones blasting from older siblings' stereos and the sweet smell of pot rolling down from the third floor.

In the summer, Mother would take the five to the pool club several times a week, or to Welch Lake once in a while for bigger excursions. I didn't register any of it. I was working two summer jobs to pay for college, or in grad school in Buffalo, coming home to visit only once or twice a year. Monica, Ilene and Julia swam on swim teams at their pool club. I saw the trophies on their dressers. After years of tap dancing lessons, Charlotte and Monica even tried out for the White Plains Talent Show, the local America's Got Talent of its day. They put on their yellow and orange satin outfits with fringe wrist cuffs and performed their tap dance for me in the living room during one of my visits home. Paul played football, won bowling trophies and hiked with the boy scouts. I heard about it all in letters, but it wasn't part of my life. Even Mother sometimes said it felt like she raised two separate families.

Yet Paul, Ilene and Julie would run out to meet me when I came home for Christmas as if I were a visiting dignitary. "Kathy's home! Kathy's home!" Paul was always the first to greet me, and I'd pick him up and twirl him around till he gave me a big kiss. He'd crawl onto my lap or squeeze in next to me on a chair. I'd tousle his blond hair and tell him about living in a dorm and eating in a cafeteria. He'd grip my hand and look up at my face. Always so glad to see me.

5. Christmas past

On Christmas mornings, for all the years that the twins were growing up, the ten of us kids woke before dawn and waited at the top of the stairs in our pajamas, our dog Charlie whining and whimpering in the excitement, until Mother and Dad went downstairs and turned on the tree lights. When they gave the go ahead we all rushed down to the living room and opened our presents in a frenzy of ripping paper and squeals and barking and the beeping and clanking of new toys. Someone put Christmas music on the record player.

O little town of Bethlehem
how still we see thee lie.
Above thy deep and dreamless sleep
the silent stars go by.

No matter how depressed Dad got or how much trouble the teenagers got into, Christmas was a day of truce, a day to remember how fun life had once been.

We older girls helped Mother fix a big breakfast of bacon and eggs that we ate in the dining room. The candles on the Advent wreath, changed out from their pink and lavender to red in honor of the day, blazed all morning. There were too many of us to go to church together, so those who hadn't been to Midnight Mass drifted off to Mass in twos and threes.

From noon on, Christmas changed over to the twins' birthday. Following family birthday tradition, Ilene didn't have to help with dishes or set the table. Both she and Paul got to laze around in the living room and ask other people to bring them a soda or a glass of juice while they played with their new toys or watched some old movie on TV, which they got to pick. At

39

dinner, while Dad read the gospel from the Christmas Mass, Paul and Ilene got to relight the red candles on the Advent Wreath. Mother carried in the roast beef with great ceremony and placed it in front of Dad, and the twins got their pick of the roast – they usually chose the ends, valuable mostly because there were only two of them – and they were served first. Our ten sequined, red felt Christmas stockings hung from the dining room fireplace mantle. Above them, the little brass angels of the Swedish chimes, pushed by the rising heat of little candles, clanged against bells as they swung by. We each had our assigned places at our long dining room table. Parents at the ends, older ones on the sides, Monica near Mother so Mother could cut her meat and rescue her from falling off her chair if she fell asleep at the table. One twin at each end.

Christmas 1961. Paul in highchair,Mother, and Mary Grace with cake, Monica in background

There were rules for everything. Pass to the right. Take the bowl before you serve yourself. Keep the side dishes moving. No one eats till everyone has been served – except the birthday kids, who could start whenever they wanted, after saying grace, of course.

Christmas, 1970. l to r Katherine, Julia, Pat, Sheila, Mary Grace, John , Charlotte, Monica and Paul in foreground with our dog, Charlie

Dessert was always the same – two layer-cakes in the shape of a Christmas tree, one white, one chocolate, both of them made from Betty Crocker mixes and decorated with green frosting and little globs of red, blue and yellow frosting made to look like Christmas tree ornaments. After the dinner plates were cleared away, Sheila, Mary Grace or I would go out to the kitchen to light the candles on the cakes. The twins would squirm and grin kitty-corner from each other at the long table. When we gave the signal, Johnny or Patrick would turn off the lights and start the singing and we'd deliver the cakes by the light of all the candles.

We all sang happy birthday with great gusto, Sheila and I adding in alto harmony, Dad wiggling his wiry red eyebrows, holding one hand to his chest and one arm out to the side, like an opera singer. Ilene and Paul were given presents wrapped in birthday wrapping paper. (*No* Christmas wrapping paper allowed.) And they got the first slices of cake, usually big end slices with lots of frosting.

I was rummaging through old albums one day, looking for pictures of Paul before he got sick, to put on his bulletin board at Westledge, and I came across one from 1970. It was the annual Christmas Eve pose of the ten of us kids, smiling in front of the Christmas tree, taken not long before everything totally went to hell. There was Paul in the front, Charlie draped over his and Monica's laps.

What happened to you, Paul? Where did you go? You'd be 11 years old tomorrow in this photo. With your wavy, blond hair and clean, soft skin, you look almost angelic. Were there devils in your head, even then?

Who was this little boy? What kind of man might he have been?

I studied the snapshot with a magnifying glass, examining Paul's eyes, his mouth, his chin, looking for tell-tale signs. Was there something we should have noticed? Was there a secret message somewhere, like the "Paul is dead" message recorded backwards in the Beatles album?

Six years later, in the spring of '76, he sprinkled his brain with Angel Dust, shaved his head and ran out of the house screaming. How long before this psychotic break had he already left for Never Never Land?

I pictured Dad after Paul was committed, shoulders slumped, playing endless games of solitaire at the dining room table, cursing his fate, disappointed he hadn't been a better provider, unable to figure out how he could have recovered from the layoff in Geneva, and confused about his wild teenagers, who smoked pot and refused to go to church. And the unthinkable: his pride and joy was in a mental hospital.

I was not a problem, of course. I was the second child, always trying to smooth things over, never any trouble.

I dreamt I dwelt in marbled halls
with vassals and serfs by my side
And of all those assembled there,
that I was the hope and the pride,

as the old Irish song goes. Like most second-born, though, I have often been disappointed. "Ah, Sheila, you must be such a help to your mother," visitors and relatives would say. And "Ah, John, you'll be a priest or doctor someday. You'll make your parents so proud." Neither oldest nor oldest son, I was invisible, pretty not beautiful, smart not the smartest, someone most people forgot about or didn't notice, including Dad.

Determined I would find a way back to a better life like I'd had in Geneva without depending on anyone, I left home and made my own way through college. I married and kept a neat home and began working on an MBA. But I wasn't paying attention to Paul.

How could anyone have seen this coming, I asked myself, over and over. Researchers tell us that it's all in the genes. A blink at conception. A strand of DNA goes a tiny bit off and the zygote is doomed. Over-zealous neurological housecleaning at adolescence sweeps away needed connectors along with childish excess pathways. Or perhaps too many are left, leaving victims with imaginary friends and hallucinations. No one really knows. No one knows how to stop it. But as I looked at the picture, studying it for the telltale signs that just weren't there, I knew I'd always wonder if there wasn't *some*thing we could have done, before it was too late.

6. *Scalped*

1972. A drunken, reeling, 12-year old Paul disrupted my wedding reception.   He and his buddies found the bar unattended at our back yard gathering and emptied a couple of bottles. His slurred speech and staggering walk didn't register, at first, as drunkenness. Until he fell over on the lawn, I assumed he was making fun of some drunken adult guest. We were a family of drinkers and smokers, so there were plenty of drunken adult guests to imitate.

As far back as I can remember, my parents had puffed and chugged their ways through a couple of packs of Pall Malls and three or four double bourbons every day, including during most of my mother's nine pregnancies. While Mother was expecting Paul and Ilene, the smell of alcohol turned her stomach, she said, and for those eight months she abstained. She soon picked up where she had left off, though, and she and my father never missed a cocktail hour for the next thirty or so years. Neither did many of their children, except to occasionally indulge in a little pot.

As the 70's progressed and Paul went from elementary school to middle school, we older ones graduated from colleges and joined the Peace Corps, signed up for Grad School, worked at archeological digs, volunteered for missionary work, and scattered to Buffalo, Binghamton, Montana, California, D.C., and Texas. Any place but home. One by one, protesting the war, questioning our religion and our culture's mores, running from Dad's vitriol, scratching for sanity as well as a living, we all left. We hardly saw or talked to each other except at Christmas; we got our news through Mother, the hub of our ten spokes.

Grandma, Dad's mother, had moved in with us a few years before, when the riots in Detroit destroyed her neighborhood and she could no longer make it on her own. But she hated depending on her daughter-in-law, of whom she had never approved. She would haunt the upstairs during the day, writing letters and looking through old photographs, descending only at dinner time, when her son had come home from work, or perhaps to fuss over Paul if Mother wasn't home. It was with his lonely mother that Dad began to spend his evenings in the kitchen. They could watch TV and sit away from the rest of the family but still in a central spot, lurking like angler fish in the shadows, ready to pounce on the unsuspecting child who might happen by.

When I was still living at home, I had avoided the kitchen after 10 pm, with its haze of bourbon and cigarettes. And I made sure I went away to college, picking a small school upstate that I could afford without any financial help from my parents. Many of my nine siblings were not so elusive and would get sucked into late night arguments with Dad about politics or religion, cursed for their mistakes, chastised for whatever small indiscretion they didn't hide from him.

Perhaps because I got away before his decline started in earnest, when I think of my father today I can also picture a young, red-headed man from the wrong side of Detroit, goofing off with old high school buddies at a big cocktail party my parents must have given, the life of the party, singing in a lusty Irish baritone, flirting with Mother's friends as they stood around the baby grand piano in the living room. Or the young father, crawling on a floral patterned carpet with three or four of us kids hanging on him, as we call out, "Tickle me, Daddy. It's my turn; tickle me!" He makes silly faces at us at dinner, wiggling his ears and scalp, affectionately calls us bird brains and knuckleheads. He shows us proudly around his office in Geneva.

But this was not the father Paul and the little kids knew.

I remember hearing a ruckus in the kitchen one evening when I was still in high school. A couple of us ran to see what was up. Sheila had just told Dad she had flunked out of college, and he had slapped her. She was standing there holding her cheek, a startled look on her face.

"You're such a failure. Ah, you've been nothing but a disappointment to me since the day you were born," Dad muttered in disgust. And then, noticing his other cowering children lurking in the shadows across the room, "You're all failures, every one of you. I feel like a failure every time I look at you."

1975. Visiting New York with my husband and baby daughter, I found Paul acting drunk half the time. He was angry one minute, laughing at something in the shadows the next. I was told he was having arguments, even fist fights with neighbor kids. I was worried. I assumed he was getting into the older ones' pot, and I asked them to hide it from him. They swore he wasn't into their stashes.

But Paul was Dad's golden boy. Star of the junior high football team, straight A's, he was handsome, funny and sweet, although no longer on the team for some reason. With his fair hair and blue eyes, Paul looked more like Dad than Johnny and Patrick, who were dark haired, like me.

He was close to Grandma, Dad's mother, who hovered over him, fixing him snacks, straightening his hair, touching his shoulders. That didn't last, of course. On Christmas Eve, 1975, she collapsed, and Paul said he found her trying to crawl up to her bedroom.

Paul says Grandma died in his arms.
He felt her spirit leave as he carried her up the stairs.
The girls were wailing where she had collapsed,

46

Mother was calling for an ambulance.
Dad hovered on a lower step,
waving his hands like a symphony conductor.
"Gently now, she's not a sack of potatoes!"
But Paul says Grandma was already gone.
"I know because her spirit spoke
to me as it slipped by."

He confided this news to me
twenty-five years after the fact,
in the visitors' lounge of Rockland Psychiatric Hospital
just moments after demonstrating
(palms pressed against his brow,
eyes and mouth a Halloween grimace)
how a famous neurosurgeon had squeezed
little, tiny, baby Paul right out of the top of his head.
"You won't have to worry about
that brat anymore!" he promised.

"What did Grandma say?" I asked.
And he just looked at me
with those sky-blue eyes and laughed.
"I couldn't hear her. Ain't that a killer?"

"But I still carry her here," he said,
and he pressed his hand to his heart.

***

1976. By the time of Paul's first psychotic episode, John was in med school and was married, living in Galveston. My husband, daughter and I were living in uptown New Orleans, where my husband was a professor at Tulane and I was looking into the MBA program. Sheila was working in Binghamton. Patrick was off in Montana or Alaska, we weren't quite sure where. Even Charlotte and Monica were off at college. Ilene and Paul were finishing up their junior year in high school; Julie still at the junior high. Grandma was gone. Mary Grace was living in an apartment in White Plains and working on a double major in Chemistry and music at Manhattanville College. Mother was giving sewing lessons and helping shoppers pick out patterns and fabrics at Stretch-N-Sew, a fabric store nearby.

That spring, Paul and his buddies Archie and Billy were skipping school and hanging around the old abandoned light rail tracks, out near Mamaroneck Avenue. Pot, hash, booze, angel dust, any smoke or pill or liquid that promised a high went down the hatch. Mother screamed and pulled at him every morning to get up. "Get hold of yourself!" she'd yell. "You have to go to school."

She drove him to school when he missed the bus. He'd wait till her car drove around the corner and sneak out to meet his friends.

Dad had another drink. "No driver's license till you bring up those grades."

The grades never made it up. There was never a driver's license.

It was early May. Mother was trying to hold her remaining family together. Dinner in the dining room every night. Grace before meals. Pass to the right. Napkin and left hand in your lap. No elbows on the table. Masterpiece Theater on PBS Sunday evenings. The family gathered round our living room TV every week to watch the mini-series, "The Last of the Mohicans."

One night, Paul wouldn't come down from his room for dinner.

"Fine. He can just starve. Pass the potatoes." Dad said.

And then Paul came running down the stairs shrieking, "I've been scalped! I've been scalped." He had shaved off his long blond hair and his scalp was bleeding. Rivulets of scarlet

48

ran down his neck and stained his clothes. "They're killing all the Indians!" he screamed. He paused, surveyed the dismayed faces. "When will you learn?"

Before anyone could stop him, he had run out the back door with the keys to the Volkswagen. They ran after him and tried to block the driveway, but Paul took the VW across the side yard, leaving Ilene, Julie, Mother and Dad watching the back lights of the orange Bug bump across the uneven lawn, turn down the street and disappear into the dusk. Paul was gone.

Dad took off after him in the old green Ford LTD, but came back defeated a half hour later. Mother called the police.

An hour or two later two policemen rang the doorbell and explained that they had stopped Paul a few miles away for driving erratically. After he babbled for a minute or two, they had taken him to the local psych ward. The psychiatrist there met with our parents that evening. The next day at Westchester Medical Center, another psychiatrist, an older woman with a heavy German accent, told them Paul had suffered a psychotic break, asked them a bunch of questions, then told them, "You won't believe me right now. But remember what I'm saying. Your son is schizophrenic. He will never get better. The son you knew is gone."

"How could she say that?" Mother cried to me on the phone a few days later. "How can anyone know whether he'll get better or not? She said we shouldn't spend any money on private doctors, that it was no use."

"You have nine other children," the doctor said. "See to them. He'll be better off in a state mental hospital."

He was held for three days.

The stay extended to a week. He was transferred to another hospital.

From my house in New Orleans, I didn't know what to think. I was too broke to fly home to visit and had a job and a three-year old daughter to look after. I found it hard to believe that he was as bad as Mother said. Her weekly letters, instead of being full of gossip about friends at the fabric store or listings of dance recitals and swim meets, now skipped into events I knew nothing about – doctors, medicines, treatment methodologies. The letters tapered off.

My parents moved Paul to NYU/Cornell Medical Center, where private, expensive doctors told them the same thing the first bunch of doctors had told them. Paul had suffered a psychotic break of some sort. He was delusional, probably schizophrenic. There was no cure, but they would try to treat him, making no promises. They enrolled him in an adolescent unit that used a combination of medicines and group therapy, and tutors came to help him keep up with his classes at White Plains High School.

Sometimes he came home on weekends. Sometimes they visited him there. There was a pool table in the rec room, and Dad showed off his old street smarts – he'd been snooker champion of East Detroit before the War. Ilene says Paul got pretty good at it.

If he came home, he mostly hung around the house. The parents of his two best friends had pulled their boys out of school, so they weren't around to hang with. One had been sent to a military academy in the Midwest and the other had moved, with his entire family, to Vermont. Now into their senior year of high school, Ilene took Paul to a couple of Christmas parties held by common friends, and Paul held it together pretty well for a couple of hours, where loud music hid many conversational flaws, but he couldn't sustain it for long.

As time went by, weekends became a nightmare. Dad would yell at him to straighten out and take cigarettes away from him. Paul would steal Dad's Pall Malls and pace around all night smoking and talking to himself. Or he ran out of the house and met up with friends and came home stoned, incoherent. Mother and Dad took turns sleeping. He was sent back to NYU for another week of treatments Monday morning.

The talking to himself and violent arguments with Dad got worse. He spent hours up in the third floor bathroom, staring at himself in the mirror and making weird faces at himself. When his hair grew in, he took the kits of food dye used to color frostings and Christmas cookies from the kitchen and used up all the red color to dye his hair. He reasoned that if he only had red hair like his friend John across the street he could be as powerful as he was.

Another time, he used the yellow dye to make his hair blond again, so he could be sane again, like he was when he was a blond little kid.

"What are you doing in the bathroom this time?" Ilene asked him one afternoon.

"I'm shaving the hair off this one spot above my ear to let the voices out."

That evening, 13-year old Julie watched as EMTs carried Paul – blood streaming from several gashes on his scalp, thrashing and babbling in a language that sounded vaguely Native American, down the stairs on a stretcher and whisked him away in an ambulance, lights flashing. "Mother and Daddy wouldn't talk about it," she told me later. "I didn't know what would happen to him, or even if I'd ever see him again."

Back at home, a few weeks later, Paul was standing in front of the bathroom mirror, banging on one ear, his head to one side, like someone might do if they got water in their ear while swimming. "Someone put a camera in my head," he told Ilene. "They're stealing my thoughts."

Mother went upstairs to get him for dinner one night and found him writing his name in red magic marker in large letters all over the walls of the bathroom. PAUL PAUL PAUL PAUL PAUL

Ilene was midway through her senior year of high school, Julie in ninth grade. Social workers and state-provided

51

tutors at New York Hospital tried to keep Paul caught up with his high school classes so he could graduate with his twin sister. He didn't seem to care.

Mother found our photo albums strewn around the living room floor one Saturday morning. Paul had taken a red magic marker and colored in red hair on all the photos he could find of himself.

With Charlotte and Monica away at college, the long mahogany dining room table seemed too much for four people and leftovers. Ilene, Julie and my parents were eating dinner in the kitchen one weekend, A & P Plaid Stamp dishware sitting directly on green Formica. No one was talking; everyone was exhausted. When Paul lurched into the room late, Dad yelled at him that he should come when called to dinner, to wash his hands and sit down like a normal person.

Paul pulled a long knife from the block of knives on the counter and waved it around, yelling, "Keep away from me! I swear I'll kill you all."

The second hand on the square green clock above the sink ticked its course to the right. The green and yellow pots and pans on the wallpaper continued their dance. Everyone held their breath. Even Dad managed to keep his voice calm. It took several minutes to talk Paul down.

He just kept getting worse. There was hardly a moment when he put more than two sentences together in a way that made any sense. The insurance would pay no more.

***

Late summer, 1977. I was working as a manuscripts cataloger in the rare books department at the Tulane University Library. My husband and I were up to our elbows in sheet rock and paint, renovating an 1850's era Creole cottage in New Orleans, where he was an assistant professor of Spanish at Tulane. My daughter Charlotte attended Miss Lee and Miss Gilthorpe's nursery school. I'd be starting on an MBA degree in

52

the fall. We were pretty broke, wrapped up in the usual concerns of a 30-year-old, academic couple with money problems.

Mother called one Sunday evening. Unusual for us back then. We usually wrote letters. A phone call meant something big. I was the last of the siblings who hadn't seen Paul for a long time. Working around books all day, I'd been able to find and read a lot about schizophrenia and mental hospitals. I'd been writing to my parents with my half-baked knowledge, trying to convince them that mental illnesses could be cured, and not to put him away.

"Your dad and I would like you to come home for a few days," Mother said. "Paul is very bad, and we want you to see him for yourself."

They sent me the money for plane fare for Charlotte and me. I took leave time from the library and flew to New York a week or so later. Paul was home, *"just for a visit,"* Mother emphasized. He would have to go back to the hospital in a day or two. Dad had taken time off from work. To keep Paul busy, he had enlisted him to help cut down a good-sized, mostly dead cedar tree in our side yard. Paul mostly just stood around, letting Dad do everything. Mother and I watched from the dining room window. Grandma's spirit watched from her painted plates that hung on the wall between the dining room windows. Paul would drag one branch to the curb for pick up, then just stand around instead of coming back for the next branch. Dad stopped to lean on his rake. He took in big gulps of air and coughed; his emphysema already giving him trouble. He yelled at Paul to give him a hand.

Paul's eyes were all bleary. He looked doped up on medication. His hair had grown in darker and he'd gained weight. His profile looked more like a man's, less like a boy. "It's been over a year of treatments," Mother said as we stood there in the dining room, watching them move around in the yard. "The insurance is maxed out. We can't get another line of credit on the house. He almost set fire to it a few days ago. Not on purpose," she hastened to add. "But he chain smokes and leaves burning butts everywhere."

"He paces, paces, paces. He comes home from the treatment center and sits at the dinner table talking to himself, laughing. He doesn't seem to know where he is or who else is there." Her eyes teared up. "He's so ill. He needs to be in the hospital."

How can someone just fall apart like this?

My parents had invited each of the older ones home, in turn, to see Paul for ourselves and question why they were doing what they had decided to do. I couldn't see any other way, either. They committed him a couple of weeks later.

The next time I saw Paul, his hair was to his shoulders and looked like it hadn't been brushed for days. He told me, "You see, if I let my hair grow long again, it'll all work out. When they scalped me, they took all my brains."

7. Leaving

1981. When I moved back home after my divorce, Paul had been in the hospital for about five years. He'd had enough brains left after the scalping to manage to graduate from high school with his twin sister, by way of the courses taught at New York Hospital, but not enough wherewithal to be allowed to go to the graduation ceremony.

A couple of weeks after graduation, Ilene left home with whatever she could carry in her set of three tan, fake leather bags she'd received for a graduation present. She'd applied and been accepted to a couple of colleges, including SUNY Cortland, where Monica was a junior, but she'd missed the deadline for sending in a deposit. Mother and Dad were so strapped with medical bills, she'd hesitated asking for it. Grace invited her to move in with her in Champaign, Illinois, where Grace was starting graduate school in chemistry at the University of Illinois. She could apply to the community college when she got there. Lost, not knowing what else to do, she left.

Dad, generally depressed since losing the job in Geneva, became more so. Mother threw herself into the choir at St. Bernard's and became a color consultant at the fabric store where she gave sewing and quilting lessons. Julia, living amongst the ashes, bumbling through her last couple of years of high school, managed to graduate in the top 10% of her grade and was accepted into Bard College. But with no money and unsure of her goals, she took a year off before leaving for Friends World College a few weeks before I came east. By the time I moved in with my parents in the fall of 1981, she and her tan, fake leather graduation present luggage were at college on Long Island. By the next spring she was off on a study project in California and in the fall went to study in Kenya.

Our old home was very quiet.

In 1978, my husband, daughter Charlotte and I had moved from New Orleans to Duluth, Minnesota, where my husband would be an assistant professor of Spanish at the University of Minnesota at Duluth (UMD). I gave birth to our second daughter, Loretta, soon after the move and for the next three years studied for an MBA at the university where my husband worked. I enjoyed my two girls and my classes. The people I met were warm, the weather cold, and life was quiet.

But my husband grew distant. He'd been an Eagle Scout back in high school, and he loved camping and Indian lore. He spent winters sitting in the basement next to the wood stove doing Indian beadwork for hours every day. In the summer, he attended pow-wows with other hobbyists, dressed in buckskin as his alter ego, Frenchie the fur trader. He traded little leather bags beaded with fanciful vines and woodland flowers for soft new deer skin, porcupine needles and beaver pelts. I didn't care much for camping, or at least not the primitive camping my husband did. In late summer of 1980, though, left alone for yet another long weekend, and with Jim at a gathering only a couple of hours away, I paid him a surprise visit.

The girls and I dressed in prairie-style, calico dresses and matching bonnets I'd spent hours making from Simplicity patterns. It was a very warm day, in the high 90's, and we baked in our yards of calico. The ground, a newly mown hay field rented from some farmer, was alive with grasshoppers and ants, and the hay stubble scratched at our ankles.

It was a large gathering, at least two or three hundred people, I guessed, teepees and period-looking tents making up the center of things, a few trailers and pop up campers at the periphery. Loretta, usually a happy toddler, whined in the heat

56

as I asked around for Jim/Frenchie, whom I eventually found sitting cross-legged on the ground, engrossed in a conversation with an 18 or 20-year-old girl with a big smile, dark hair in long braids and wearing an intricately-beaded Indian maid costume. She looked much like I did when I was 20 years old, before two Caesarians and years of indifference.

Charlotte spotted him right away. "Daddy!" she shouted, and ran to give him a hug. Loretta whined. I stared.

"She's my friend's daughter," Charlotte's Daddy insisted. His friend's alter ego couldn't read or write, so his daughter wrote for him, he said. I had seen those letters coming into our house for the past year; when he said his friend's daughter had written them as his scribe, I had pictured a twelve year old. His friends busied themselves setting up a place for me to sit. One of the women got out a zinc tub and young men poured buckets of water into it so Loretta could play and cool off. "You should have told me you were coming," he said about twenty times.

I smiled and accepted a cool drink of something. Charlotte ate something. Peoples' faces were a blur. I didn't want to have a screaming match in front of a bunch of people I didn't know. I dried Loretta off. Someone gave me some talc that I sprinkled on the heat rash on Loretta's neck. We sat and there was some chit chat. After a couple of hours, the girls and I left the pow-wow. Their daddy stayed there two more days.

By the next January, Jim had moved out. And by June he'd left me in Duluth with two kids, no job, no car, and a house I couldn't sell. In 1981 Duluth was going through a big recession. There were layoffs everywhere. My ex had managed to find a new job at a college in Illinois, but he wouldn't get paid till September, so there was no money coming in except from my campus job, which paid $10 per hour and would end on Labor Day.

Without a car, I couldn't even do grocery shopping or go

look for a job. I had almost finished my MBA, but I had no credit history in my own name. I finally started crying on the phone with my sister Sheila one night and two days later Mother called and told me to come home. I defended my master's thesis and graduated. A friend of mine from the MBA program who worked at a bank helped me get a car loan. I bought a five-year old Dodge Monaco Brougham, rented out the house, packed my blue graduation-present luggage and as many boxes as would fit into the trunk of the Dodge, tied the girls' bikes to the bumper and drove east to live with my parents while I looked for a job. I wasn't thinking about Paul.

I felt trapped back in my parents' house. It was so quiet. And the child support was slow in coming. After more than ten years on my own, I found myself totally dependent on my parents. As much as I appreciated their help, I felt like I was in a sort of limbo – neither heaven nor hell – not really living, just trying to get to a spot where I could live again.

Christmas, 1982. From l to r, Steve Leggett holding son Russell, Ilene, Monica Leggett holding daughter Christine. Then Paul, Katherine and Mary Grace. In front on the right, Katherine's daughters, Loretta (left) and Charlotte. This is the first Christmas in Mother and Dad's new "retirement" home

The job search took a while. Despite my MBA, despite my applying for jobs in corporate finance, recruiters kept asking me if I could type. Mother was a great help with my two girls, who were 8 and 3. She insisted on paying for the day care center for Loretta, my younger girl, so I could be available on a moment's notice for any job interview opportunity.

Paul had been transferred to a state hospital about an hour's drive north of White Plains. When she asked me to go visit Paul with her on Sunday afternoons, how could I refuse? We'd pack a lunch and she, my girls and I would make a day of it.

"Don't worry," he'd take me aside and reassure me. "I'm really working undercover for the FBI. I'll be leaving the mental hospital when I finish my assignment. Can you buy me some cigarettes?"

We argued with him endlessly.

No, you are ill. You are in the hospital because you have schizophrenia. You do not work for the F.B.I. You were never scalped, Paul.

It was hopeless, but we called him on the crazy stuff. Look around. No one is killing Indians anymore. Look in the mirror: you are a 23-year old white guy.

On the long drives with Mother to and from the hospital, I learned that my father's father, Grandpa Flannery, had a brother who Mother thought suffered from mental illness. He died in his mid-fifties after being in and out of hospitals in Indiana most of his adult life, and all of the adults had been very vague about what was wrong with him. Grandpa had another brother who had two daughters, my father's first cousins. Cousin Wilmae Flannery had married a California man and lived out west. One of her children, a boy a little younger than me, also suffered from schizophrenia. He was one of the so-called lucky ones, the ones who were helped by medications. But he had been in and out of mental hospitals.

59

I had never known any of this.

The siblings sometimes wondered aloud which was worse, to be so crazy, like Paul, that you hardly know what was going on? Or to almost make it, get a job, find an apartment, and then relapse?

And over the next twenty years, as our children entered their late teens and grew argumentative or distant, we would wonder, was this the beginning of something worse? Or was it just normal adolescent angst? Paul at 16, cutting school and experimenting with drugs, just seemed like a teenager going through a rough time. Patrick dropped out of high school to join a band and travel. He drank too much for a few years but he wasn't crazy. Still, those defective genes were lurking just out of sight in our family DNA. How could a parent tell?

***

All through the eighties, Mother visited Paul at Harlem Valley Psychiatric Hospital almost every Sunday, often shaming me into going with her, even long after I had moved out and was on my own. If it was a nice day and we could do something outside, we took my two daughters, careful to never bring them inside the ward. My father never went. He had retired from his job on disability at age 62, a few months before I moved back east. He hardly came out of his room except to fix himself a drink or play solitaire at the largely-unused dining room table. Little by little he became a hermit. I can't remember him ever going to visit Paul.

Harlem Valley Psychiatric Hospital was located in Wingdale, New York, directly across the street from a Metro North train station. If Paul behaved himself he could get a grounds pass, allowing him to go outside and walk around the grounds. Sometimes he stayed on the grounds, sometimes he didn't. During the first few years he was there, he used to take off every now and then and hop the train back down to White Plains. The conductors never threw him off. He'd claim he had lost his wallet; they gave him a form to fill in with his name and address and sent him a bill, which ended up with Mother, who always sent back a check.

Paul sometimes hitched home, too. We often wondered about people who would stop and pick up a hitchhiker near a mental hospital. He looked pretty normal from a distance – blue jeans, tee shirt, pleasant smile. But the minute he opened his mouth, they had to know that something was very wrong with him.

One of several buildings at Harlem Valley Psychiatric Hospital. The grounds looked more kept when Paul was there. Note the bars on the windows. (With permission from Creative Commons)

We all hated going to visit. Even the outside of the place was scary. Hulking, Depression era brick buildings; many abandoned. Barred windows, something out of Dickens. If I was with Mother, she always went in to get him. If I was alone, I had to go in. The hallways were dark. Three levels of locked, gray metal doors with tiny, chicken-wired windows. At each door, "State your business. Step this way. Stay close to me," the attendant would say, ring of keys jingling, rubber-soled shoes padding quietly on terrazzo floors.

I always wondered which of Paul's ward mates needed all those levels of security. Vacant-eyed, horny, babbling in ill-fitting clothes, they paced around their olive drab day room. The smell of floor wax, cigarettes, burned coffee, of loneliness, of despair. They'd surround me, touch my sleeve, ask me for cigarettes, tell me I was pretty.

"Leave her alone," the attendant would say. "She's here to see Paul. She's his sister!"

"Can I take him out to the diner?" Sometimes they

wouldn't let him leave the ward. I hated sitting with him in there. I learned to call ahead. Yes. He had permission today. I'd sign the book. We'd burst out of the double-locked doors and I'd gasp for air.

For an excursion on nice days, we used to wander around Webatuck craft village, a few miles from Wingdale, where a cooperative of artisans had taken over a cluster of old buildings near a small dam. An enormous chair stood outside the Hunt Country Furniture Store, which sold hand-crafted wooden furniture. There was always someone taking a picture of their child up on that chair. Nearby were a glass blower, a cooper, an art gallery that sold paintings, potters, and paper and candle makers. On Sunday afternoons, many artists would be at their crafts. My daughters fed the ducks and geese at the pond above the dam.

Paul stood and looked down at the stream running under a little bridge there.

The water splashes and gurgles. A youthful, dark haired Paul and the feathered Chingachgook haunt the virgin woods along the Hudson River, where the air is clear and squirrels scold and scramble through the branches above them. Their feet sink into the cool, dark earth. A pinecone thrown to the ground in just the right way can burst open and lost Mohicans will spring up, full grown, to reclaim their birthright.

"I need some pine cones," he explained to Ilene over Easter dinner one year. "Save me some pine cones if you see any."

Paul was twenty-three, twenty-seven, thirty.

I moved out of my parents' house to my own apartment a mile or two away. A co-worker set me up with an old college friend of his; Ken and I married, and I moved twenty miles north to Bedford. Sheila put her belongings into storage, went on a world tour and met and married a man in Egypt. Grace got married to a fellow grad student at the University of Illinois. Monica got married and had two babies in three years. Charlotte served in the Peace Corps in Zaire. Pat was still somewhere up in the northwest, playing gigs in Alaska, according to his postcards. John graduated from medical school and moved with his wife and three children from Texas to North Carolina. Grace got divorced and moved to California. Ilene married, had twins and moved to Wisconsin. Sheila and Saher moved back to the States and settled in Boston.

Paul was still at Harlem Valley Psychiatric Hospital.

Whenever I went through the double-locked doors at Harlem Valley Hospital, or Hudson River Psychiatric Hospital, or Westchester Medical Center or Rockland Psychiatric Center, Paul was always just as glad as he'd been as a kid when I came home from college. "Kathy! You came!" He'd give me a hug and walk close to me, smiling and nodding.

I'd sign him out – *We'll be back in four hours*– and take him to the nearest diner and buy him some pizza or a burger. We went over family gossip. Monica's two little ones had red hair. My daughters were getting older. Ilene sent pictures of her twin boys, one blond, one dark haired, just like him and Ilene. I showed him their picture and he told me the blond haired one was a devil. "She better watch out for that one."

One day, he held his hand to his face, grimacing when he tried to eat. Several of his teeth, furry and green with neglect, were loose. At the next visit, there were wide gaps. "They took my teeth," he said. "Look: a bunch of my teeth are missing."

They'd been taken by Indians, mad scientists, secret government agents. The stories varied. He was the victim of intricate plots.

Mother talked to the doctors and case workers. How can he be losing his teeth? What's wrong here? It seemed like every few weeks he had lost another tooth. He simply refused to brush. His social worker told us they had finally sedated him and pulled the rotting stumps out. Soon he was toothless. They fitted him for dentures, but he threw them away. Twice.

And then a new theme appeared. He told us about his children, the hundreds of them, born to him from his lost teeth or magically springing to life from the earth. "They're calling for me! They're lost!" he sobbed, one day at the diner. He covered his face with his hands and lay prostrate on the table, knocking his silverware to the floor, shoulders heaving, heartbroken at the tragedy.

"There are no hundreds of children," I tried to comfort him. "C'mon, you know that."

This only made him angry. "You can't tell me what to do. I know what I'm talking about. I *know*! I pulled out my own teeth for them." Fists slammed.

"I was raped last night. I'm telling you, five of them held me down," he insisted one day.

Was that last one true? Could someone be abusing him? How could we know?

As I drove him back to the ward he'd ask me five or six times if he couldn't come home and live with me. It was the way almost every visit ended. "C'mon, it'll be fun," he'd say, "like when we were little and lived at home with Mommy and Daddy."

Giving up on that, he'd settle for cigarette money.

I'd start crying seconds after the door to the ward closed. My baby brother went back to cold tile floors, smells of ammonia and bleach, bars on the windows, lousy food. What did they do all day? He'd been such a loving little kid. But I couldn't take him. I didn't trust him around my daughters. Hell, I didn't trust him around me! So I took my turn visiting him every so often and left it at that.

8. Taking turns

From: Katherine Dering,
To: Patrick Flannery, Ilene Wells, Sheila Flannery, Charlotte Flannery, Grace Flannery, John Flannery, Laurie Flannery, Monica Leggett, Julia Brower, more...
Date: Friday, August 06, 2007 11:18 AM
Subject: Paul

The date for Paul's first treatment has been set: Tues, August 14. He will go into a three week cycle. He gets a series of daily shots, supposed to help him keep up his white and red blood cell count days 2 – 7, then the chemo. The Dr. will want to see Paul for follow up on the 20th or 21st day. The next chemo would be day 22.

I tried to ask the doctor our questions, asking if we couldn't start tomorrow. He said the nursing home would need a few days to get the prescriptions filled for the shots. So Tuesday was the date chosen that everything would be ready. He said if things get pushed back a day or two it doesn't matter. He was a little short with me.

Maybe it's me. I'm always too blunt. I'll leave the doctor talk to Monica.

Monica had asked about a treatment called ablation therapy, and he said that it was too much to go into, but it was only available in a clinical trial, and he didn't recommend Paul for such a trial. He doesn't fit the profile.

Johnny will be with us at the follow up visit. Maybe he'll be able to ask the right questions. At least, since he's a doctor, they won't blow him off.

A few of us will be taking Paul out for a boat ride on the 12th on the Hudson. He is on an oxygen

concentrator now, like the one Dad had. He doesn't
need it absolutely all the time, but he is apparently a
little low on oxygen.
       I hope he'll be able to do the boat ride.

With all Paul's mental problems, we hadn't really
thought about physical ones. If we worried about anything, it
was about who would care for him when he got old. Now, with
his cancer diagnosis, we were all consumed by a feeling that this
was it for him. We wanted to do something for him now, take
him somewhere maybe, before he got too sick from the chemo.
But where? No one wanted to be responsible for him for more
than an afternoon. Half the siblings lived too far away to be of
much help. John, a doctor now, lived in North Carolina; Grace,
in California; Sheila in Boston. Even the New Yorkers were
scattered in different counties. No one was closer than an hour's
drive.

Email became our war tom-tom. Suddenly we were on
the phone or sending group emails to each other with a flurry of
ideas ranging from a weekend at the Jersey Shore to a day at
Welch Lake, where Mother used to take the little kids years ago.
But after about fifty emails, Ilene said he'd always liked boats
and he used to love hiking in Bear Mountain State Park, so we
looked for ways to take him on a boat ride on the Hudson that
sailed past there.

I never really thought about what Paul liked or wanted
until now. He wanted out, mostly. Out of the mental hospital.
Out of the adult home. Out.

I tried to rent a boat for an afternoon, afraid that Paul
would act up on a public trip. But I had no luck. Not in our price
range, anyway. We settled on a big day cruiser that took a
couple of hundred passengers on a three hour run from
Peekskill, north a mile or two past the Bear Mountain Bridge,
then back to Peekskill. We'd cross our fingers.

66

A bunch of us met at the docks, the local stalwarts. The river gleamed like polished silver and in the midday heat, the hills glowed in a kind of turquoise haze. We'd brought coolers of food and soda, and the snack stand on the boat sold hot dogs and ice cream.

l to r, back row: Ken Jr, Shelley, Pat, Paul, Ilene, Julie, Katherine, Charlotte, Ken, Jennifer   Front row: Monica, Zach, Katie, Alex

Paul greeted each of us as if he were the host of a big party. He kind of swaggered. "Hey, glad to see you. Great day, huh?" Once we'd all settled in, he took a seat by the railing on the top deck and hardly took his eyes off the shore. He smiled and looked more relaxed than I'd ever seen him. I think it was the smile. He hardly ever smiled like that. He looked so normal.

"He was in the Boy Scouts back in White Plains," Ilene told me. A friend from our church was the scout leader and used to take Paul and his friends camping at Bear Mountain. "Before Paul got sick, he was trying to get a job working for the

U. S. Conservation Corps," she said.

I didn't know that. I knew almost nothing about my little brother. And I noticed Ilene said "before Paul got sick." I usually said "before Paul went crazy." I couldn't imagine Paul thinking about a career. When I left for college Paul was only six. I hadn't lived with him as a teenager. I felt more like his aunt than his sister.

He was a baby. I blinked. He was delusional.

Siblings, nieces and nephews took turns slipping over to Paul's bench and spending a few minutes visiting with him. No matter what you said to him, he sort of chuckled and nodded. He hummed and kept his eyes on the shore.

Julie's daughter and my two grandsons ran around chatting with other passengers. The green hills slid by and small pleasure boats put-putted up and down the river around us. A train ran along the east shore, a silvery caterpillar in the sunlight. Paul told us stories about Indians on the hillsides and his experiences back when he was Clint Eastwood. They put in long days doing movie shoots on location.

We broke out the snacks and sodas. The boat slipped under the Bear Mountain Bridge, a gleaming arch high above us. I'd lived near the Hudson River for thirty years and this was the first time I'd done a river cruise. Paul drank his Diet Cokes and grinned for three hours.

A couple of days after the cruise, Monica and I settled

68

into our new chauffeur duties like it was something we'd been doing all our lives. At home, Mother made us all take turns at everything. It was Sheila's turn to wash and mine to dry. Or it was my turn to vacuum and Mary Grace's to dust. As we went through high school, we fought over whose turn it was to use the phone or borrow the car. Now Monica did two days, I did two days, and we flipped the fifth when necessary. Pick Paul up, take him to the doctor or the diner. If there was no medical visit on my day, I might take him to the park or we'd wander through stores in downtown Peekskill. Sometimes there was a movie playing I thought he might like. Or we wandered through the Walmart. "Do you need anything, Paul?" (other than a new brain or new lungs?)

Ilene, Julie, Charlotte and/or Patrick did weekends. Out-of-towners filled in as needed.

From: Monica Leggett
To: Laurie Flannery, Ilene wells, Katherine Dering, Grace Flannery, Sheila Flannery, Patrick Flannery, Charlotte Flannery, Julia Flannery, more...
Date: Wednesday, August 15, 2007, 11:23 AM
Subject: Paul's first chemo
          Hi Everyone,
   I will try to convey the fiasco of the first chemo day, though I wasn't there for any of it. Katherine and Patrick are both working today. The good news is that I spoke to Paul's nurse this morning and he is up and walking around like nothing happened. No complaints of pain or nausea. But the whole process took 13 hours to complete!
   He didn't leave the nursing home till 12:30 (delay due to bed availability. Medicaid will pay for chemo only if administered in a hospital, apparently). They started with a blood test to see if he was OK before the chemo, but it took hours for the results, then talk with his Dr. to OK the process, then order the meds from the pharmacy,

---

69

then start his IV. He didn't start the anti-nausea IV until 5pm and the chemo started at 6:15. Katherine was with him from 12-6pm. By 5pm she was reminding the nurses that he needed his normal psych meds. Two hours later when he told a completely bizarre story to the nurse about his successful operation, the nurse finally got one of the meds but not his Haldol. That took another reminder and a call to the nursing home and his doctor to get the prescription to the pharmacy. What a complete and utter lack of continuity of care! Ken took over at the hospital from 6-8pm and Patrick took the very late shift of 8-1:30. He brought Paul back to West Ledge and got home at 2 A.M. Thanks to Katherine, Ken and Patrick.

I'll talk to you all soon. I'm on my way to Westledge now. It takes me 90 minutes to get there, so feel free to call me on my cell if you have any ideas or suggestions.
Monica

We spoke to Dr. Ayan's office, to see if in the future, Paul's first blood draw could be at his office, where they could get the results in 15 minutes. The doctor could then order the medications right away, cutting at least 4 hours off the process. We also asked him to order Paul's afternoon psych meds in advance because no matter what time in the morning Paul got to the hospital, he'd still need his meds by 5pm. Even with a good scenario, he probably wouldn't be on the nursing floor before 11am and the three IV's took 6 hours.

We picked up a rhythm, Monica and I. The hospital and doctor's offices were within blocks of each other and the nursing home. We got to know all the delis and diners, which waiting rooms had comfortable chairs, which doctors always ran late. We didn't see each other, because we saw Paul at different times; our conversations were by email. But between phone calls and overlapping visits, we talked or emailed pretty much every day.

A month went by, two months... Paul was biopsied and scanned, chemo-ed, radiated and nebulized by a United Nations of oncologists and radiologists and technicians and nurses from Pakistan, India, Jamaica, Russia and Ireland. We seem to have outsourced health care of our poor to immigrants from the countries where we outsource everything else. Contrary to the oncologist's fears, none of them seemed to have a problem caring for Paul.

But as I made the forty minute drive to and from my home and Westledge, *I* was still wracked by questions. Why were we trying to save him? Who benefited from extending his life? At his worst moments over the years, we had sometimes mused that it might have been better if he had died that day of his first psychotic episode. Paul's mental illness was a sore that wouldn't heal. If he survived this, would he go back to another one of the awful group homes, wandering aimlessly around town with nothing to do, no purpose to his life? He was helpless and foul-mouthed much of the time - or at least inappropriate - a drain on society. What was the point?

Yet he was my brother. If I even mentioned such thoughts, Ilene and Monica said I was all wrong. If he could just live another five years, or maybe ten years, scientists might discover the cure. About two thirds of all schizophrenia patients are helped dramatically by existing medications. Maybe the next one would work for him.

From my home in Bedford, I would head northwest to the village of Katonah. From there, I drove west on Route 35, which wound along, widening to four and five lanes near car dealerships and big box stores and then narrowing back to two lanes through residential neighborhoods. Rainy days, sunny days. The road made a 90-degree turn at the foot of the Amawalk Dam, which holds back reservoir water that is part of the New York City water system. Sometimes a fountain there sprayed a mist high into the air. It made me think of the *jet d'eau*

71

in Geneva. There was a turn in Yorktown near the K-Mart. I missed it once in a while, preoccupied by my thoughts.

Autumn arrived, red, gold and dry. Paul was getting chemo every three weeks.

I often found Paul in the common area at the end of the hall where patients gathered some afternoons. Pass the beach ball. Sing along with old songs and an enthusiastic volunteer playing an electric keyboard. Most of the other patients were tiny, mummified-looking old women who, when not watching the beach ball fall to the floor, sat in wheelchairs outside the door to their room staring off into space. They rocked baby dolls and helped an activity coordinator fold clean cloth diapers. There were only a few men in the facility. Paul liked to chat with the orderlies there.

He was losing weight, his hair fell out, and still, he'd slip off his nicotine patch to sneak a smoke outside with the orderlies, who gathered near the garbage shed at the back of the Westledge property.

"My man! How's it goin'?" They'd exchange various handshakes.

"Yeah, I played football in junior high school for the St. Bernard Bernies, and I got whacked in the head," he told them. "I've just never been the same since." He smiled and shrugged. *A simple smack and look what happened. Life's such a crap shoot.* "Gotta light?"

(He did play football; he likely got whacked more than once. After all that's been in the media about pro football players developing dementia, I sometimes wonder if there wasn't some truth to that.)

Meantime, his doctor ordered an ankle bracelet that would set off alarms if Paul went out the door.

Paul and his roommate, John, shared a double at Westledge. It wasn't a large room, but it was comfortable and clean, with matching blue-striped bedspreads and drapes, the nicest room Paul had in the thirty years since he was committed in 1977, only 17 years old. There was a wide window that looked out over the circular front drive. Each resident had his own TV and remote, as well as a built-in dresser, a wardrobe, and a bulletin board. John's family had posted a few get well cards and photos. We copied family photos and posted them on Paul's board.

1971 Back, l to r: Dad, Mother, Sheila, Monica, Charlotte, Katherine, Mary Grace, John, Patrick. Middle, Grandma and Grandpa Lesperance. Front, Julia, Ilene, Paul

My daughter-in-law Jennifer, my stepson Kenny's wife, made a photo album for Paul with pictures from the boat trip. Monica added a few photos from some Thanksgivings and Christmases. Paul liked looking at pictures of himself.

A long curtain ran on a ceiling track and you could pull it through between the two beds for privacy, like in a hospital room, but it was hardly ever pulled, unless a doctor came by.

John's daughter brought him food from home and sat by his bed trying to feed him. "Eat, Pa, eat," she cajoled. "You can't come home if you don't eat." She'd have lasagna or meatballs or ziti with melted cheese, sometimes homemade soup. Her father would turn his back to her and curl up into a tiny ball and pretend to sleep. She shared the extra food with Paul. Paul loved lasagna and meatballs.

The minute his daughter left, John, a wiry little guy, got up and wandered the halls, but he fell repeatedly. I arrived one day and he was in a wheelchair like the mummy ladies, sitting at the door to their room, his arm in a sling and a big bruise spreading across his cheek. I said hello. He smiled but didn't recognize me. His dementia was progressing rapidly.

"Please, John, stay in your chair. We'll take you for a walk if you want. Call us with your call button," the aide would say. John would nod. A few minutes later he'd get up and fall again. The aides clucked and smiled sympathetic smiles. They hummed and joked as they made their rounds in their rubber soled shoes and suggested to the family that they sit with him to keep him still.

9. Visiting Days

From: Katherine Dering
To: Grace Flannery, John flannery, Kerry flannery, Laurie flannery, Michael Flannery, Patrick Flannery, Sean flannery, Sheila Flannery, Monica Leggett, Ilene Wells, Julie Flannery ... more
Date: Saturday, October 6, 2007 8:48 AM
Subject: Paul update

I visited Paul twice this past week. He continues in very good spirits. He loves his DVD player, his new bedspread, and his photo album. I found him going through the pictures while watching a James Bond movie.

He is looking a little gaunt. There is a skull -like look about his face. Johnny says that may be due to muscle wasting. Let's all remember to bring him high protein treats, like Boost or Nutrament or other milk-shake-like high protein canned supplements. Bring a paper cup, as well, as he seems to have some difficulty drinking out of the can.

We strolled around the river front park and watched the trains and the boats. Then sat at the train station cafe near the water and he had a big burger and we just enjoyed the beautiful day.

In mid-October I took Paul to the oncologist's for a pre chemo checkup. It was time to begin his next chemo cycle.

Paul was waiting at the nurse's desk for me, eager to leave the facility. He liked riding in the car. A left, a right, a short drive, then a left into the parking lot. He seemed relaxed in the doctor's waiting room, which was jammed, as usual. I think he was getting used to the routine. A nurse called him in for blood work. He went in without a fuss, but I tagged along anyway. Then back out to the waiting room.

Many of the other patients were grey-haired couples. I wondered which of the two had the cancer. I suspected the man. I don't know why, but it seemed women brought their husbands for doctor visits; female patients came with their sister or friend. I brought magazines, but Paul didn't like to read. By the end of the 45 minute wait, he was restless. He cranked his arm where the blood had been drawn up and down like a pump, and he fiddled with the bandage at the elbow.

Finally, we were called into the doctor's office. More waiting. Paul paced.

The doctor swept in as if by a strong current. "Your blood work indicates everything is fine," he said.

Paul sat and nodded, his hand holding his chin as if lost in thought.

"We'll do this chemo, then if all goes well, we can start radiation shortly after that."

Paul jumped to his feet. "No," he announced. "I've had enough chemo. And I don't need radiation," he shouted, enunciating each syllable for maximum effect. "The cancer is gone. I know it is. I passed a mass *this big*" – his hands indicating something bigger than a basketball – "out my ass". You should have seen it." This last part he confided as if some sort of secret.

The doctor pulled his head back into his neck like a turtle into his shell and blinked.

Paul went on and on about it, insinuating that the doctor was making up all the cancer information, describing the cancer he had passed. "I know it's gone. I saw it," he repeated. The doctor blinked again. It would have been funny if Paul hadn't been so upset.

"You're just feeling nervous," I said.

But he was picking up steam now. "You need to make your money. I understand that," he said. He held up the imaginary basketball-sized turd again. "But it was this big, I'm telling you. The cancer is all gone."

Why did he do this? All nice, nice with us, then antagonistic with the doctor.

I watched Paul. The doctor watched me.

Paul's rant finally dwindled off. He sat quietly for a minute.

"What do you say, Paul? Shall we let the doctor get on with what he has to do?" I asked.

Paul let his hands rest in his lap. His turn to blink. He gave a reluctant nod.

The doctor approached him tentatively to take his blood pressure and listen to his chest. "Now breathe." Paul took a breath. "Again," he said. Paul cooperated.

The doctor rummaged through his papers then looked at me and cleared his throat.

I picked up the message. "Paul, do you want to take a walk around the parking lot for a couple of minutes while the doctor and I talk?"

"I'll wait by the car," he said, and hurried out of the room.

The doctor explained that before radiation could start, Paul would need another PET scan. Only then, assuming that it indicated the cancer had shrunk as expected, would we need to make appointments for the radiation. "I thought it might be better if you told him about the PET scan," he said.

"The first couple of radiation treatments will be long ones," he explained. They would involve a couple more CT scans of some sort, to identify exactly where the remaining tumor(s) were and what angle to shoot the radiation. After that, the radiation visits would be short, but would have to be interspersed with two more chemo treatments, most likely.

The nearest radiation facility was a couple of towns over, in Mahopac. But Paul might not be able to get the radiation there because it was not associated with a hospital and Medicaid would only pay for hospital care. If so, it would have to be done at Westchester Medical Center in Valhalla, through an outpatient facility they had. That would be a *huge* circle drive, from home to Peekskill, down to Valhalla, up to Peekskill, then back home, over 100 miles each time. Every day for six weeks.

"But let my nurses see about all that," he said. "For now, you and your sister just get him to the chemo and the PET scan."

I found Paul outside near the car. He was growling at the doctor again. I figured he was hungry - I could recognize the signs now - and took him over to the Ecuadorian bakery across from the Salvation Army store to pick up some pastries and coffee. But Paul saw the menu board and asked if he could order the shrimp salad sandwich on a croissant. "Sure," I said. "Whatever you want."

"I love shrimp," he said. We sat at a small table and Paul wolfed down the sandwich while I sipped my coffee. It was very strong.

I wondered how often they served shrimp at the mental hospitals he lived in. At the Chinese restaurant nearby he always ordered shrimp egg foo yung.

When we got back to Westledge a nurse and a couple of the orderlies were coming out the front door, leaving for the day.

"Hey, man, what's happening?"

"My man!"

"How's it going, brother?"

Paul had to shake everyone's hand. "Not too bad," he answered. "Can't complain. I was just out with my sister."

"I see that. That's cool, man."

I nodded and smiled at these men who were such a big part of Paul's daily life, so thankful they were good to him.

"Have a good day," they said to me.

"You, too," I answered.

Paul and I took the elevator up to 3. An array of silent old ladies sat in wheel chairs in front of the opening elevator doors like most days, watching the doors open and close with blank looks.

If we had no doctor appointment I sometimes brought along my little Maltese dog, Buddy. We'd take him down to the park and he barked and chased the gulls and pigeons. At the nursing home, he put his paws up on one woman's lap one day and she smiled, the first time I had ever seen any reaction from her. She lifted her hand a tiny bit and moved it over to stroke Buddy's paw and said, "I had a dog once."

I waved and said hello. I always wondered if she would talk again. Not today.

I dropped off a couple of cans of a chocolate flavored protein drink with the ladies at the third floor desk, to save in the refrigerator for later, then got Paul settled in his bed watching a James Bond movie on his DVD player (one with Roger Moore as Bond of course.) A pink-flowered kalanchoe had appeared on his window ledge in a bright yellow glazed clay flower pot. He couldn't remember who brought it. As I left, he leaned back against his pillows, eyes closed.

10. The Great Emptying

Pink flowers, yellow flower pots, sunny window ledges.

The patients at Paul's nursing home were not wealthy people. Yet with whatever they paid via Social Security and Medicaid or Medicare, Westledge managed to appear clean and bright. It was a low rise, blond brick building with big, plate glass windows facing a broad circular drive and bordered by flowering shrubs. Its cheerful yellow forsythia and daffodils that were blooming when Paul moved in, in April, led to the pale pink of saucer Magnolias and the deeper pink and red of tulips and azaleas in May. Tall hardwoods gave dappled shade in summer. In the fall, specimen maples turned brilliant red. Inside, visitors were greeted by a homey reception area furnished like your grandmother's ideal living room, with striped wallpaper, oriental style rugs and overstuffed, pastel floral-upholstered couches with brass table lamps on the end tables. Nurses, attendants and social workers smiled and asked how they could help.

Worlds away from most of the places Paul had lived in.

When I moved east in 1981, New York State had already begun to empty and close all the state mental hospitals. This wasn't unique to New York; it was a national trend. Beginning as a trickle, the great emptying had become a torrent by the mid-1980's. The United States had 340 public psychiatric beds available per 100,000 people in 1955; by 2005 there were only 17 beds per 100,000. Much of this shrinkage in capacity at psychiatric hospitals during these years was a result, direct or indirect, of the introduction in 1954 of chlorpromazine (Thorazine), the first effective antipsychotic, which made it possible, for the first time, to control the symptoms of schizophrenia and thus discharge some patients.[1] Paul was on this medication for many years. But the number of people still needing hospitalization did not shrink as much as the hospitals did. Experts today estimate the U. S. still needs about 50 beds per 100,000 people to care for those suffering from the most severe forms of mental illness. With a population of 310 million, that means the United States needs 155,000 psychiatric beds but has only 53,000. Those seriously ill people have no residential setting to care for them.

The excessive zeal to release all mental patients in the seventies and eighties had as much to do with funding and misconceptions about the causes and treatment outcomes of mental illness, as it did with the new medications. By the mid-1980s, the doctors treating Paul were well aware that a biological component was primary to the disease. It was a misfiring in the brain; the wrong messages were getting through. But despite the rapidly growing body of knowledge that pointed clearly to biological, neurological causes, old stereotypes persisted.

At the onset of Paul's illness in the 1970s, psychologists still tossed around terms that blamed the mother in some way. Although falling from favor, the terms "smothering mothering" and the "schizophrenic mother" were bandied about in pseudo-scientific literature. Sometimes mental illness was blamed on repressed homosexuality or an oedipal complex – Freudian beliefs still popular in some circles. And in many people's heads it was linked to the sufferer's own sinful ways or to some God-assigned stigma.

Because of the many false beliefs, insurance companies were permitted to set lower lifetime limits for expenditures on medical care for mental illness and higher co-pays – often 50%.

---

[1] "The Shortage of Public Hospital Beds for Mentally Ill Persons", A Report of the Treatment Advocacy Center, E. Fuller Torrey, M.D., et. al., www.treatmentadvocacycenter.org

This is how my parents reached the point that they could no longer afford to care for Paul themselves.

Meanwhile, well-intentioned do-gooders, as my father called them, had sued New York State to close down the huge state institutions, made infamous by investigative reporting on places like Willowbrook, on Long Island, where developmentally disabled people were being mistreated. Medicaid reimbursement schedules[2] were written to withhold payments to large mental institutions, accelerating the closures nationwide. Trying to make sure the bad patterns were not simply replicated in new buildings, new laws called for smaller, more humane, community-based residential facilities for patients needing long term care.

One by one the hospitals closed; a few homes were built for people with Downs Syndrome and the like, but no one

---

[2] When Medicaid was passed into law in 1965, it took on from the states about 50% of the burden of caring for indigent people like Paul. A little known part of that law was something known as the "IMD exclusion." Medicaid will make no payments to any institution for mental disease, or IMD. An IMD is defined as any facility of more than 16 beds where more than 51% of its patients between the ages of 22 and 64 are being cared for by reason of severe mental illness. Nursing homes caring for elderly Alzheimer's patients are not impacted, nor are institutions caring for young patients suffering from mental retardation or illnesses. In 2014, as part of the implementation of the Affordable Care Act (ACA, or Obamacare), demonstration projects in 15 states have temporarily lifted some of the IMD restrictions. The results of this effort will not be known for some time.

While this may have been meant to ensure that mental patients were not warehoused in huge institutions, in practice it made it impossible economically for state facilities to care for the people most severely afflicted with diseases of the brain. Not only is a facility precluded from being reimbursed by Medicaid for the individual's day-to-day care, but individual patients' eligibility for Medicaid is canceled while they are inpatients in an IMD. Consequently, to receive treatment for medical disorders not related to their severe mental illness, they must be discharged from the IMD, have their Medicaid eligibility reinstated, be treated in a medical/surgical setting, and then be readmitted to the IMD. In other words, it is virtually impossible. See http://www.nami.org, the website of the National Alliance on Mental Illness.

wanted crazy people in their neighborhood. Almost no smaller facilities were built for people like Paul. The shrinking population of those suffering from serious mental illness rattled around on a few floors of hulking, ancient hospitals, many of them built a hundred years before as sanitariums for people with TB. The rest were simply released, often to slumlord-operated single room occupancy buildings (SRO's) and adult homes, where they were still confused and unable to care for themselves and now had no supervision. The streets of New York and other big cities suddenly were full of mentally ill homeless people wandering around, sleeping in doorways, dying of exposure or getting arrested. Eventually our prisons filled with mentally ill people who, only twenty-five or thirty years before, would have been humanely cared for in an institution. [3]

Every time there was a story in the papers or on TV about one of them, Mother cringed.

A mentally ill man pushes someone off a subway platform; a mentally ill

Paul and Mother, about 1985.

[3] The nation's jails and prisons are turning into warehouses for the mentally ill, with the three largest jail systems housing more than 11,000 prisoners under treatment on any given day. And the problem is growing, according to a report September 25, 2013 in The Wall Street Journal.
"In every city and state I have visited, the jails have become the de facto mental institutions," Esteban Gonzalez, president of the American Jail Association, an organization that represents jail employees, told The Wall Street Journal.
The jails in Cook County, Ill., Los Angeles County, and New York City have the largest populations of mentally ill inmates, the Journal noted. The estimated 11,000 prisoners being treated daily in the three systems alone equals 28 percent of all beds in the 213 state-run psychiatric hospitals across the country, according to statistics from the National Association of State Mental Health Program Directors Research Institute.

homeless person wanders the streets of New York City pestering passers-by, is killed in a bar fight, is found frozen on the streets. Mother would steel her mouth into a thin line. *This will not happen to my son. I couldn't stop him from going mad, but I can try to make his life as good as possible, within its limits.* She volunteered at the hospital library. She stopped by the ward on non-visiting days. *My son is not alone,* her presence said. *I am watching.* She joined NAMI, the National Alliance on Mental Illness, a new organization which advocated for both patients and their families. Her focus was always on making the remaining hospitals comfortable for Paul. We couldn't imagine that he would ever be released.

Determined to keep her son safe, Mother stayed tuned in to public hearings and release meetings – sort of like parole hearings – at the hospital. She showed up for all of them, ready to insist that Paul stay hospitalized. "You can't just release him. Transfer him to a nicer, smaller place, yes. But I can't handle him. He'll set fire to the house. He'll get into bar fights. He'll hurt someone," she told anyone who would listen. She wrote letters to our Congressman and State Assemblyman.

Mother made the one-hour, forty-five mile drive up Routes 684 and 22, from White Plains to Harlem Valley Psychiatric Center so often, she could recite every gas station, restaurant, fitness center, farm, antique shop, motel, bank, diner, lumber supply store, army surplus store, church, fast food joint, office park, bakery, school, ice cream stand, car dealership, nursery and garden supply store along the two-lane state road.

She made sure we included Paul at all our family gatherings, making the long drive to pick Paul up for Christmas and Thanksgiving dinner herself, and ferrying him to my house or Monica's for the afternoon. My house was about halfway between Paul's hospital and Mother's home in White Plains. She would visit Paul in the early afternoon, then stop off at my house for dinner. Her Sunday visits to Paul and me became a ritual.

***

A few months after I had moved back east, my parents had moved from the Philbrick house to a smaller one, a ranch style home to which someone had added a second floor with three more bedrooms and an extra bath. They lived on the first floor, but had rooms upstairs for any of us who needed a place to stay, like my girls and I did, and later, my sisters Charlotte and Julie did. One room was designated as Paul's, but he never slept in it. Mother kept a wooden box of his high school memorabilia in the room's closet just in case.

Dad went up to inspect the second floor once, before they moved in, and he never went up again. He had retired on disability at age 62 with chronic pulmonary problems, although I always thought he suffered as much from depression as lung issues. By 1982, though, and for the last six years of his life, he was tethered to an oxygen concentrator for advancing emphysema. He could shuffle from the bedroom to the family room to the kitchen, his long, green oxygen hose trailing behind on the green carpeting and the beige kitchen linoleum. His hair, ever finer and thinner, eventually hung in wispy white locks that grazed his shoulders. He seldom left the house. He had his liquor delivered by the case.

He would sleep till four or five in the afternoon. A quick bowl of Rice Krispies and a banana with a pile of pills. A brief pause, to watch The Mike Douglas Show or Live at Five, then time for a highball. And another, and another. He'd sit at the kitchen table watching sports games and reruns of detective shows on a small black and white television and playing solitaire from five in the afternoon until four or five in the morning, living only the flickering half-life of the cocktail hours, sipping, cards slapping, flipping channels as Johnny Carson or Kojak reruns took up where the ball game left off. And as the evening progressed into morning, he would progress to writing

85

neat lists of injustices, or schemes for riches on his yellow legal pads, all the while mumbling vague, rambling tirades, cursing his luck at having such a cold, judgmental wife and such poor excuses for children. In the midst of long, painful-sounding coughing fits, you could sometimes hear his osteoporotic ribs crack, buckling him over in pain. Eventually he'd stagger off to solo unconsciousness.

One night, he slipped while reaching for the ice tray, and the next morning Mother found him flopping helplessly on the kitchen floor, a white, flaccid blob in a shallow pool of water, gurgling incoherently, hip shattered. After a few weeks of rehab (for alcohol withdrawal as well as the new hip) he was back to his accustomed spot: yellow legal pad, neatly sharpened pencils, playing cards, overflowing ashtray, Merits and his highball close at hand.

He became such a hermit, no one really missed him when he finally died in 1988. The house was just a little quieter without the whooshing noise of the oxygen concentrator and the quiet slap slap of the cards on the Formica table.

Paul didn't seem to notice. Dad had hardly even visited Paul for years.

* * *

1988. The year Dad died, Patrick came home from Montana. For more than a decade he'd been drinking and living the rock-n-roll life while traveling with his band in the Northwest, but he arrived for Christmas dinner at my house that year sober, wearing a cowboy-style shirt with mother of pearl-covered snaps and a string tie. It was great to see him after so long. Even Johnny made it up to New York to visit that December. We played loud music all afternoon and I hurt my ankle dancing the Soupy Shuffle with Johnny in the den. He and I used to watch Soupy at lunchtime back in Detroit.

Paul began scowling at Pat over appetizers. While everyone was up in the family room for our annual Yankee

86

swap gift game, my husband, Ken noticed Paul wasn't with us and went looking for him. He found Paul sitting on the kitchen counter next to a half-empty bottle of Vodka, mumbling and making faces.

"So what's happening Paul?" Ken asked him, trying to reach for the bottle.

Paul turned to him, scowled, and growled out, "That Patrick. I hate the fuckin' guy. He's killing all the Indians!" He made a fist. "I outta kill him!"

Ken whisked away the bottle. Someone took Paul outside for a walk and a smoke, and within a few minutes Mother was driving him back to the hospital with a plate of food and his birthday cupcakes. We thanked the fates that Paul still had a place to go.

We knew the hulking institutions were horrible places to live, but as awful as they were, we feared his release. He saw fellow patients leaving. He constantly begged us to take him home with us. But how could we? Caring for him would be a full-time job. Among the siblings we had accountants, a teacher, a doctor, a social worker, a therapist, a software specialist, and a consultant. We struggled at our jobs all week, tried to find time for our spouses and children evenings and weekends. There was no way he could live in my home, with my teenage daughters. I could do my four or five visits a year and be done with it.

For now, for me at least, Paul was safely stored away in a locked mental cupboard labeled "crazy relative." Despite the push to release everyone they could, Paul was still cared for. And who knew? Doctors might be able to help him one day. Besides, he was Mother's problem, not mine. I could take care of my family, see friends and go to work like nothing was wrong.

11. The Ground Shifts

1993. My secretary interrupted me in a meeting to tell me I had a phone call. "The EMT's just left with Mother," my sister Charlotte said. "She collapsed at the foot of the stairs in the front hall. I heard her bang against the railing and ran over. She looked so bad. Julie went with them."

I was working as the chief financial officer of a little bank in Connecticut at the time. My sisters Julie and Charlotte and Charlotte's husband and baby were living with Mother while Julie applied to grad school and Charlotte and her husband looked for a new house.

Mother was 71 and healthy, or so we thought. She was always out and about, busy with Paul, her choir, friends and the fabric store. She was just home from her 50th college reunion in Detroit. She had collapsed? This didn't compute.

The part Charlotte told me about Mother still being in her bathrobe at 10 am didn't really sound like her. But I knew the schedule she had been keeping lately, and we had often told her to take it easier. But then Charlotte told me that Mother hadn't felt up to working on the *Times* crossword puzzle this morning. This was not like her, at all.

"You know Mother. She thought it was just bad heartburn from her usual three cups of black coffee," Charlotte said. "But then she collapsed, so I called 911."

I heard a gurgle. She was crying. "I've never seen her like that before. She was so pale." She sniffed and cleared her throat. "Anyway, they just left. They were using their sirens and everything."

It took me almost an hour to get to the hospital. As I

made my way into the emergency room alcove Mother's eyes opened. "Katherine!" I think she might have smiled. Leads were attached to her chest, sending out regular, reassuring beeps to the bedside monitor. I kissed her on the cheek and took her hand.

She was feeling OK, she said, "except for this awful weight on my chest. It feels like a big, heavy brick."

I could see that she was shivering under the thin blanket. I asked the nurse to bring her another one. She brought two. I felt their warmth; they had been heated. I tucked them around Mother's shoulders and she closed her eyes and purred like a cat. All those years of her tucking us in; I don't think I had ever tucked her in before.

The machines beeped and buzzed. The room smelled of alcohol wipes and disinfectant. The visitor chair was small and hard. Julie paced around and went out to ask, again, for a cardiologist to examine her. Mother opened her eyes, and I could tell she was staring at my suit. I immediately knew what she was looking at and found myself apologizing for wearing brown.

For years Mother drove the family crazy, making us "have our colors done" to determine our "color season" so that our clothing would be the right shades at all times. At the fabric store where she worked, they assigned customers to color seasons in order to help them pick out the right fabrics for their sewing projects. Customers paid to be draped in various shades of fabric while other women commented on whether the *drapee* looked good or *all washed out* in the different colors. Mother got into the concept with a passion. Once she'd been labeled a "summer," Mother had thrown away every item of clothing she owned that did not conform to the rules. She expected all of us to do the same thing. She threw out my father's favorite brown sweater, an act he never forgave her for until the day he died. I was apparently a winter and was told to wear clear dark or bright colors like black, navy and bright blue-red, with clear white for contrast. Never yellow, never brown or beige. "Don't you always want to look your best?"

I had almost delayed getting to the hospital by about half an hour to go home and change into something navy blue before I got here.

"I know. I know. Brown's not my color," I now felt obliged to say. "But the suit was on sale and I wanted a change."

She smiled weakly. "No, actually, it's all right. The suit is dark enough, and the white blouse gives good contrast."

The blouse was beige. Now I was really worried. It was not like her to cede on color issues.

Outside the curtain we could hear ER personnel talking. Carts rolled by and nurses called out blood pressure numbers and doctors called for tests. Julie and I paced and fretted. Nurses drew blood and asked questions then disappeared.

I talked with Mother's doctor from the phone at the nurse's station. Finally, after several hours, they agreed to admit her to the hospital, "just for observation," they said. "Her EKG looks normal," they kept saying, as if that completely negated that awful pressure, that huge brick sitting on her chest.

She was moved to her own room, where it was much quieter and the bed was softer. She dozed off a little. We called her internist again. He called a cardiologist who finally came by late afternoon. They didn't think it was a heart attack. "It may be her gall bladder," he proposed.

Her friends, Mrs. McGovern and Mrs. Murphy stopped by. "The girls are asking about you, Mary Kay. They send their prayers." The afternoon dragged on.

Mother tried to smile from time to time. Like Jackie Kennedy. I remember the way to make Mother happiest was to tell her that she looked like Jackie. She did her chestnut brown hair in a smooth bouffant, just so. She had dark brown eyes, and plucked the inside of her eyebrows above her nose to give herself that wide-eyed look Jackie had. No longer was Mary Catherine Lesperance the little girl from the farms of Windsor, Ontario, striving to fit in with the sophisticated Detroit girls. She was Mary Kay now. Pall Malls and highballs. Bridge and cocktail parties. Coffee, never tea. Trips to Europe. She wasn't a country girl any more.

"The doctors have her scheduled for some tests in the morning," a nurse informed us, looking around disapprovingly. "And remember, she's only allowed two visitors at a time."

Afternoon moved to evening. We took turns getting something to eat downstairs. Meatloaf and mashed potatoes with gravy, a watery Coke. Julie left to watch Charlotte's baby so Charlotte could come by. My husband stopped by with my younger daughter, Loretta. They sat with Mother for a few minutes, then left to join the other siblings gathering at Mother's house.

And still, the unrelenting chest pain.

Finally, Mother's eyelids kept closing. The hospital had begun to take on that nighttime cloak of muffled, secret noises. A nurse's padded footsteps. A creak as a door opens down the hall. Visitors heading home. Brief snatches of mumbled conversation before a door swings shut.

The phone rang, just as Charlotte was leaving. Our sister Monica was so concerned. It was her son's birthday, so she had stayed home for him. "I was thinking I could drive down to visit in the morning." Sheila was driving down from Boston tonight, and should be in White Plains soon, she told us. And a message from our brother Patrick. Could he come by now?

"Tell everyone to let me have some rest," Mother insisted. "One at a time. They can come in the morning. It's too much. You're all too much for me." She closed her eyes.

Mother's friend Joan and I sat with her few minutes longer. Joan didn't want to let go of her hand. "We'll go now, too," I finally said, "and let you sleep." I brushed my lips against her cheek. It felt soft, like a paper tissue. But dry like tissue paper, too, or like onion skin. No moisture, no pinkness, no life.

"Try to get some rest." I said. Mother leaned back into the pillows with a pained look and closed her eyes again. "I'll try," she said. "I'm so tired."

"I love you, Mary Kay," Joan cried. "Don't leave me. I'll be back as soon as they'll let me, in the morning. Don't you dare leave me. I'm counting on you."

"I'll come by and check on you in the morning, too," I said. "I gave the nurse my number. She can let me know if you need anything."

Morning never came for Mother. She died that evening, about 30 minutes after I left. A burst aortic aneurism.

We were all stunned.

***

McMahon's Funeral Home on Mamaroneck Avenue reeked of lilies.

The out-of-towners had all arrived. Paul was due any minute. The people at Paul's hospital were very good about helping us with him. We all agreed he should come, but wondered how he would behave. How would he react to seeing Mother's body? Would he make a scene?

His attendants led him into the room, and Ilene ran over to him right away. He was dressed neatly in a tweedy gray sweater and baggy black chinos. His hair was combed, he was clean-shaven, he didn't smell, and his sneakers were tied. Ilene led him to the casket and he walked right up to it and stared at Mother's body closely. He spoke quietly, only insisting on touching Mother's face again and again, commenting that she was stiff and cold. But he didn't cry at all, much less make a scene. I cried enough for both of us.

The two attendants were the only Black people in the

room. They seemed relaxed, though, as if this were easy duty for them. After Paul stood up front for a while, they escorted him to the back of the room, one on each side, and the three sat like piano keys in the folding metal chairs that had been added to handle the large crowd. Family friends stopped to chat with him. I have no idea what he said to them. I kept waiting for him to create a ruckus. We were all relieved when he was taken back to the hospital.

On the morning of the burial, once the family had all filed past one last time, the undertakers pulled a curtain across the front of the room so that we couldn't actually see them close Mother into the coffin. The funeral home director looked expectantly at us, motioning for someone to join him behind the curtain. Sheila, who had assumed the mantle of senior Flannery, calling herself our "auntiarch," hurried to comply.

Sheila was an archeology major years ago, and she believed it was important to send people off to the next world with the things they considered most important in this life. When Grandma Lesperance, Mother's mother, died several years before that at the age of 94, the funeral director arranged rosary beads in her hands. Sheila hid some Kleenex into Grandma's sleeve and a little baggie of pink Canada mints alongside her in the coffin. Grandma had never gone anywhere without them before. Why start now? I watched with squeamish fascination at Sheila's nonchalance, touching Grandma's dead body. I was glad Grandma would have our offerings with her for her journey, but I would not have been able to be the one to place them so close to the body.

I never was very good about death and dying. Maybe it was going to our cousin, Patty Blake's wake when I was eight. All the grownups sniffled around the coffin, where she lay so stiffly in her First Communion dress. I think she'd died of polio. I'd been in the same hospital, down the hall from her with pneumonia just a week or two before. I don't know how nurses

93

and doctors and undertakers deal with their jobs.

Now Sheila again took charge of Mother's funeral offerings. She slipped a worn old deck of bridge cards, the last *New York Times* crossword puzzle Mother had worked on, a ballpoint pen, and pictures of Mother's eleven grandchildren into the casket before it was closed. Then she gathered up Mother's jewelry on behalf of our entire clan. She waved the bag of booty for me as she emerged from behind the curtain: Mother's mother ring, with its ten garish semiprecious birth stones; her seamstress watch with a scissor for the hour and minute hands; and her string of 10 pearls. As she picked up her coat from the chair next to me, though, she started to cry. Not one much for hugging, I managed to pat her on the back. She looked up, appreciatively, and we walked to our cars.

I zombie-walked through all the Catholic funeral fol-de-rol. I hadn't been to Mass since college and had raised my daughters outside of any religion. I found it hard to believe in the Christian afterlife and found the repeated references to resurrection and salvation tedious. But the rituals were familiar-the same songs, the same readings from my childhood. And anyway, it was *what you did.*

While friends and relatives swarmed Mother's house after the burial, some of my sisters and I went for a walk and I noticed that realtors were holding an open house at the house across the street. I had been named executrix of Mother's estate and, thinking ahead to selling her house, I wanted to check out the competition. As we approached the house, someone wondered out loud if we'd need a story to explain why we were looking together.

At the funeral mass, the priest had called Mother determined. She was *determined* to care for her large family, especially her troubled youngest son; she was *determined* to raise us in the Church; and so on. We decided to tell the realtor that we were an order of nuns looking for a new convent and called

94

ourselves the Sisters of Perpetual Determination. That's what we wrote on the realtor's sign-in sheet. It stayed a family joke for years.

I sold Mother's house and the assets were distributed among the ten of us. In accordance with Mother's will, Paul's $1/10^{th}$ share was placed in a trust, with me as trustee. The money was intended for when he got better, one day. As executrix and trustee for Paul, I became the family's de facto business center. In thanks for my efforts, the siblings gave me a plaque inscribed to me as "executrix extraordinaire, with gratitude from the sisters and brothers of perpetual determination."

***

The pomp and ritual of the Catholic funeral ceremony stayed with me for weeks. All the music and vestments and genuflections. All the talk of God and salvation.

I was as religious as any of my relatives when I was a kid. As I grew older, I found Catholicism a mish-mash of altruistic but naïve spiritualism and archaic ritual. Still, they were *my* archaic rituals; I was used to them. I could have put up with it for the familiar sense of belonging, but something had snapped for me in college. The role of women in the Church was so low, the celibate priesthood and their proscriptions against birth control and divorce so out of touch with the realities of a world facing overpopulation and where men mistreated and abandoned women in droves, leaving them to care for unwanted children that I decided to just bag the whole thing. I didn't feel any need for some priest in a strange outfit to anoint me with oils or give me forgiveness for anything.

And religion was shown at its weakest with problems like mental illness. Why would a just god, if there was one, visit such a curse on a young boy like Paul and his family? Why does *anyone* become mentally ill?

Modern theories of causes centered on genetic anomalies. Yet his twin sister was fine and the other eight of us, with the normal range of problems, seemed to be firing on all cylinders. Why Paul? Was it brought on by drug use? Or had he used drugs to self-medicate? If the development of Paul's brain caused it to misfire, if he couldn't tell the difference between random thoughts and reality, if he would never get better, who

Monica, Paul & Katherine 1996

was he? What were we supposed to do with him? Our religion had no answers.

And then, about a year after Mother died, someone realized that no one had visited Paul in months. Not one of us. We had brought him to the first Thanksgiving and Christmas after her death but then nothing. It was almost Thanksgiving of the next year when we realized we had made not one trip to the diner, not one visit with a care package, hadn't taken him to a movie or bought him a pizza since the new year. Nothing. There, I've admitted it. Weren't we the shitty siblings?

Before, everything went through Mother, but now we were disorganized. We hardly felt like a family anymore. Sheila was in Boston, Johnny in North Carolina, Ilene in Wisconsin, Grace in California. We didn't call. We didn't write.

Poor Paul! His mother, who had visited him every week for 16 years, was dead. He must have wondered what had happened. Had *we* given up on him? Would he *ever* leave the hospital again? I can hardly imagine how abandoned he must have felt. Pacing from window to window, caught up in any one of his delusions - phantom children crying, scalpings, FBI interrogations.

Before Mother died, if she couldn't visit, she'd call one of us and ask if we could please visit him, and we did. Now, no one was asking. Everyone assumed someone else would go. We weren't asking each other. We hardly even communicated except on the holidays.

Horrified with our own thoughtlessness, we agreed that we would take turns. We brought him to Thanksgiving and Christmas. I said I could do primary contact for a while, at least. The others in the area would help when they could. It wouldn't be every week, like Mother had done, but we would let Paul know we cared.

12. Shapeshifter

Paul was a shapeshifter, a skinwalker, a Navajo witch, able to spot another witch no one else could see. He had powers none of us could understand.

Shapeshifters can change shape in an instant. Some Navajos believe that if you make eye contact with a skinwalker, your body will freeze up with fear and the skinwalker will use that fear to gain power over you. If you ever lock eyes with a skinwalker, he can absorb himself into your body. [4]

He could be the dutiful child with Sheila; aggressive hunter with Patrick and Ken; kind uncle with small nieces and nephews; and a wolf with most young women, including me, despite my age.

The first time I visited with Paul after mother died, I took him to the Eveready Diner near the hospital. It was crowded, and Paul and I had to wait a while for a table, then wait several minutes more for service. Cutlery scraped on china; a screaming two-year old stood on his seat and cried to go home; dishes clattered as careless busboys dumped them into large plastic bins.

Paul sat directly across from me at a small table. He'd

---

[4] The phrases in italics are taken primarily from Newsvine and Wikipedia, two open sourced on-line reference pages, mixed liberally with general knowledge from years of reading Tony Hillerman. See: http://ghall1950.newsvine.com/_news/2011/05/29/6743126-native-american-legendsshape-shifters-skinwalkers; also, Wikipedia.

been in a good mood when I picked him up, smiling, happy to be out in the fresh air. But as we waited, he became convinced that the man at the next table was staring at him. He started mumbling, turning away from the man and then turning quickly to catch him in the act of staring.

The best sources for a witch's power are the corpses of children, especially twins.

Paul needed to be alert at all times to protect himself. He kept looking around the restaurant at the other diners and making faces, stretching his mouth wide, then pursing his lips. I got out family snapshots to show him, but he didn't seem interested. He peered out of the far corners of his eyes till his eyelids flickered. He whispered to someone I couldn't see.

When the food arrived, Paul grinned and dug in. He slurped down his burger and fries in a couple of minutes, happy again, then stared intently at me as I munched on my B.L.T. Suddenly he said, "I bet you don't know that I have the Power." He waved his hands in front of him and wiggled his fingers like a magician.

I looked at him, trying to figure out where he was going with this.

He raised his right arm, brought it level with his shoulder, and made a gun with his thumb and forefinger.

"One zap of my gun at one of your big tits, and you'll be in sexual ecstasy," he said. "With just." Pause. "One." Longer pause. "Zap."

He took aim at my chest.

"Zap!" he said.

I felt his eyes bore into me like razors.

He'd learned this trick in FBI training, he explained, to help him ferret out information, while working undercover at the mental hospital.

"Stop it, Paul. Let's try to have a nice lunch today, okay?" I looked down at the rest of my sandwich, sighed, pushed it away.

All around us, patrons in T-shirts and sundresses laughed and chattered as they munched on their burgers and BLT's.

Paul's fingers, stained yellow from years of nicotine, tapped nervously on the black Formica table, his long legs churned back and forth like dough forks, underneath. His hair, flecked with a bit of gray now, fell into his eyes. He ran his fingers through it, leaving it standing on end, then leaned his six-foot frame over the table and played nervously with the sugar packets.

The wolf was gone.

"What I want is a cigarette. Why can't we sit in the smoking section?" His voice rose till he was shouting.

"Hush!" I said, looking around. "There is no smoking section anymore, Paul. Don't start. People are staring at us."

He leaned back, jutting out his chin and squinting, peering through narrow slits at the other diners. He turned and opened his eyes wide and scowled. I felt his eyes bore into me again. He was concentrating his powers.

I took another sip of my soda. The ice had melted and it tasted watery.

"Why don't you go out and have a cigarette?" I said, handing him a pack of matches. I watched out the window till I saw him walk through the parking lot to its grassy edge. It was a gray November day; the trees were bare. He had already lit up, and he stood with his neck hunched into his shirt collar, smoking and looking through the trees down to the river.

A wolf prowling his haunts along the river, a coyote howling at the wind.

Our waitress hovered expectantly nearby in her pink nylon dress and too much hair spray.

"Check please?"

She pulled it from her pocket.

I delivered Paul back to his ward with relief, and I cried all the way home.

***

One Christmas, a few minutes after munching on crab English muffins and raiding the bowls of candy kisses, Paul lunged at my husband in the kitchen and pinned him against the wall.

"I oughtta kill ya!" he said with a snarl, choking Ken with his shirt collar.

"Naw! You don't want to do that," Ken said. "I'm your brother. You don't want to kill your brother!"

Paul thought about that for a minute. "Yeah, I guess you're right," he said, shuffling his feet in an "aw shucks" move.

Ken hid the knives, and someone tagged along with Paul for the rest of the day.

***

My daughter Loretta, about 18 at the time, was peeking into the Christmas stockings. Paul came up behind her and said in a hoarse voice, "I could rape you right now, you know."

Thanks, Uncle Paul. Merry Christmas to you, too.

***

Paul acted differently with each of us. Sheila said he never gave her a hard time like he did with me. But he was even worse with Monica and Ilene. At least I could stare him down and he would eventually stop. When Sheila announced to us all that she'd take a turn being the primary contact for a couple of years. I was happy to defer to her. After the zapping incident, my husband came with me a few times, or I tagged along with Sheila, but otherwise, I tried not to be alone with him anymore.

With a shapeshifter, you never know where or who he'll be next.

101

13. Release

The first time I went to visit Paul after we agreed to step up our visits I had trouble finding him.

Harlem Valley Hospital had closed about a year before Mother died and Paul had been moved to Hudson River Psychiatric. An institution just as hulking and almost as old as his old place, his new home was somewhere in one of eight or ten old buildings that sat on a hillside looking out over the Hudson, just north of Poughkeepsie. Mother had visited him there many times. In nearly two years, I hadn't even been there; I'd seen my brother only on the holidays.

The buildings were mostly institutional red brick, with peeling beige paint around the windows and bars on some. A nine-hole golf course was spread over the grounds, a remnant of the hospital's heritage as a turn of the century sanitarium for the well-to-do. A couple of men strolled along, pulling their bags of clubs on little carts behind them. I eventually located a map of the grounds and found Paul in one of the older buildings, in the second most restrictive ward. The only place worse than his was the ward with convicted murderers and rapists. Double-locked doors that creaked and clanked, chicken wire in the door windows, bars on the outside windows, worn couches in the day room, the smell of disinfectant – it was all too familiar.

"Kathy! You came! Where have you been?" he asked. "Were you away? I thought you must be in Africa or something." He laughed. No reproaches. Considering that Sheila, Julia and Charlotte had all been in Africa not that long ago, I was pretty impressed by his focus. I looked at him, and he just grinned. Who was he today?

Before we could go out, the staff insisted I tour what they

called the self-sufficiency facility. Administering the release programs over the past several years, they had found that many patients were afraid to leave. Some of them had been living in an institution for thirty or even forty years. Most had been abandoned by their families and hadn't been in a private home for a long time. Even if patients were being helped by the new medications and were more in touch with reality, they didn't know how to navigate independent living. They had never set an alarm clock or bought groceries for the week. They had never cooked a burger on a grill or decided when to take a shower. The hospital had set up a simulated apartment in the basement, where residents were taught life skills like how to boil water, fry an egg, and change the sheets on a bed.

As we strolled through the basement set-up, which didn't look at all like an apartment to me, I could tell that the staff was quite proud of it. Each room was twice normal size, with double wide doorways to accommodate wheelchairs and large groups. But it had a typical home bathroom with a tub and single sink, as well as common items like clock radios, table lamps and a residential size stove and toaster oven. Our tour guide talked about time management skills and cleanliness habits. We nodded politely.

When we were halfway out to my car, I asked Paul, "So how are you doing on all that life skills stuff?"

He started laughing, shaking his head. "I have absolutely no idea what they're talking about," he said. "Are they crazy?" He held his belly with crossed arms and laughed till he cried.

So much for him being connected.

We were all relieved that they hadn't released him while we were so inattentive. I guessed that even the most zealous of the anti-hospitalization people realized that he was too ill to be out on the streets. Except for the talk of self-sufficiency training, his treatment at Hudson River didn't seem that different from

Harlem Valley Hospital.

As Sheila took on the primary visitor role after the zapping incident, she decided that she would sort of adopt him. "I don't have kids and all that, so I have more time than most of you," she informed us. She'd drive down from Boston on a Friday morning and visit Paul, sometimes chat with one of his caseworkers, then visit me or one of the other sisters. My youngest off to college, I had some free time on the weekends, and on Saturday Sheila and I would head down to the Metropolitan Museum of Art for a day of R & R. Mid-month, the rest of us filled in with visits to Paul from time to time.

But our visits weren't as consistent as Mother's had been, and we didn't attend any family meetings. We were visitors, not advocates. And one day, about three years after Mother died, Patrick arrived for a visit and found out he was too late.

Pat called me one Thursday evening and said, "Guess where I am." He was at Paul's new digs, he said. And this time it was different. Paul hadn't just been moved; he'd been released. A hearing had been held. No one showed up to protest Paul's release, and he had been discharged from the hospital. He was no longer a ward of the state.

How could they do this? Paul was obviously out of touch with reality. He was usually clean, since the hospital had a laundry, but his hair was alternately shaved off or long and tangled, depending on his mood. Sometimes he said long hair gave him power, but next month it might have all been shaved off. He still talked about the FBI and Indians all the time. And he could shift from happy to scowling and ranting in an instant, with no provocation or warning.

Where was he being released *to*? Where would he live? None of us could take him into our home. We couldn't be on alert all day, 24/7, like we'd need to be. But if we didn't take him, what would happen to him?

The thing Mother had been so afraid of had happened. I

felt like we had let her and Paul down.

Patrick gave me the location of the half-way house Paul was staying at, and on my next day off I approached the building with some trepidation. I hadn't visited Paul alone since the zapping incident. And I wasn't sure I was even in the right place. The directions put it on the grounds of the recently closed Harlem Valley Hospital, which was now being engulfed by tall weeds. This building was on the far periphery of the grounds and looked like a very large farm house, with a big screened-in porch across one side. The grass around it was mown and litter-free. There was no sign.

A pleasant-faced man in blue jeans came to the doorway "Yes, you're in the right place," he said. He asked a young man, another resident, to get Paul. "Your brother is in his room. I think he's sleeping. He'll be down in a minute, though. He's looking forward to your visit."

There was a clatter on the stairway and Paul burst into the room. "Kathy! You came!"

Paul showed me around like a tour guide at an historic cathedral. The downstairs had large rooms with wood floors and big, overstuffed furniture. An uncarpeted wooden stairway led up to seven or eight bedrooms. Paul shared his with Marty, a young man who had been his roommate at Harlem Valley and Hudson River. Their room looked like someone had tossed it; there were clothes everywhere. But Paul seemed pleased with it. "I'm supposed to wash them," he informed me. "They're going to show me how tomorrow." He laughed a wheezy laugh. "I really have no idea," he said, shaking his head.

He led me downstairs and had me sit with him for a while on the large screened-in porch. The furniture was heavy duty and well used, with cigarette burns everywhere you looked, but it was comfortable. Wide, overflowing ashtrays took up most of the tables. "I can come out here and have a cigarette whenever I want, even during the night," he explained, grinning. He patted the couch. "Try it out," he said. So I did. "This place is great."

We checked out the kitchen, a sprawling, farm-house style affair with old wooden cupboards. Curling beige linoleum exposed the wooden floor, below. The giant wooden table had at least a dozen chairs. "Just like our table back home in White Plains," Paul said. The social worker on duty showed me a sheet of paper tacked to a kitchen cabinet, listing jobs and who was assigned to do them each week. Setting the table, clearing the table, sweeping up, helping to unload groceries... Paul would be assigned a duty soon. Eventually, he took on sweeping duties and was quite proud of it.

Mike ran me through what would be Paul's new routine. Paul and Marty had been released from the hospital; they were free men. They could live wherever they wanted to live, but if they chose to live here, and they were encouraged to do so, they had to obey the rules. Every Monday through Friday, the house ran vans to take the residents to their hometown for day programs. Paul and Marty went to White Plains, to an out-patient psychiatric clinic, a forty-five minute drive. Paul would be monitored here at Haven House, but the degree of choices and responsibilities he'd been given constituted a huge change from his life on the ward. Mike explained that Paul would be expected to help decide on menus, keep his room clean, etc. Paul began fidgeting while the house manager and I chatted, pacing and sending glaring looks. Nervous in his new place, I guessed.

"Sorry, Paul, I don't have to talk with Mike like this," I said, and cut the conversation short. "Let's go out."

Paul settled into the passenger seat and played with the window. "I thought for a while you had forgotten me," he said as we drove. He was very quiet.

We found the diner we used to go to with Mother when he was at Harlem Valley before. While waiting for our meals, I asked him if he was looking forward to being assigned a chore there.

"I told you all about that," he said. "You just don't understand." He explained *again* – when will we learn? – that his gums had sacrificed their teeth to give birth to ghostly children, hundreds of them, who sprang up and disappeared forever. He mourned their loss.

His eyes filled with tears. "They're crying for me, Kathy." he told me. He stopped eating to press the palms of his hands against his ears as if to keep out the noise, or to keep his head from exploding from the screaming. "They're crying for me." He grimaced. "Can't you hear them?" he shouted.

I managed to distract him by talking about ice cream for dessert. He calmed down and finished his burger. He cheered up as the meal hit his system, and he pointed out the window to the route he now took to walk to the diner where he sometimes spent some of his own money to buy a cup of coffee by himself.

"I can just come and sit here whenever I want," he said. He blinked and looked around smiling, as pleasant and calm as if he hadn't just suffered through crying children for the past half hour.

A skinwalker can change shape in an instant.

I couldn't shake it off so easily. I dropped him off and got stuck in a half hour of stop and go traffic on Route 22. When I merged onto Route 684 and the traffic cleared, I speeded up and almost instantly heard a police siren and saw flashing lights in my rearview mirror. I was so startled I almost swerved into a ditch. I had whizzed right by a cop.

I pulled over. Great, I was thinking. The perfect ending to a perfect day.

My heart was pounding like it would break out of my chest as the trooper approached my car. He was a young guy, maybe 25 or so, with a bland, clean-shaven face, a silly, broad-brimmed state trooper hat and a uniform with lots of badges.

He said something about me driving erratically, checked out my license and registration, and asked where I was going. I burst into tears.

His face fell. He said, "What seems to be the problem, ma'am?"

I babbled for five or ten minutes about how my brother wasn't getting better, that he would never get any better, that you'd think there would be something doctors could do for him, and on and on, sobbing the whole time. I told him about Harlem Valley and Hudson River and Mother dying and ghostly children crying. He said he thought they had closed Harlem Valley Hospital. I told him about Haven House.

Cars were whizzing by on Route 684. We were near an overpass and the roadway shook whenever a truck went by. The trooper stood there chatting with me until I had stopped crying. It was late afternoon, and it was beginning to get dark. The western sky took on a lavender color.

I felt totally exhausted.

"Now, why don't you just sit here for a while and relax," he said. "I'm not going to give you a ticket or anything. But use your turn signal if you change lanes, okay? And maybe you could stick to the speed limit the rest of the way home?"

And then he tipped his hat. He actually tipped his hat! And just before he walked away, he said, "I'm real sorry about your brother. It's real good of you to look after him."

Driving home I practiced deep breathing. My eyes had that swollen, after- a-crying-jag feel. The move to Haven House was a big change. No wonder he was so agitated, I thought. Twenty years of scheduled, meals, activities, bath times, whatever, were now over. But it looked like they would take good care of him there.

Poor Paul. Nearly all of us had faced our own demons, at one time or another. But the family's anger and resentment, addictions, fear of failure and wishful thinking had all seemed to settle on him, the apex of Dad's desires. He was the hero with the tragic flaw; and we, my siblings and I, a Greek chorus, were able only to stand on the sidelines and warn and lament. Paul embodied both our childhood faithfulness and our adult disconnect, all in one sloppy package.

In the next few months, we'd find Paul wearing blue jeans full of big white splotches and little holes, evidence of a laundry day bleach mishap. More often, Paul was dirty looking and smelled of BO. If he refused to do his laundry no one would do it for him and no one would force him into the shower.

But there were plus sides to the new ways. Once a week, if the residents did their chores and hadn't earned too many negative points, they got to go on a ride to a nearby mall, where they could walk around on their own, maybe buy a soda at the food court. The group sat together in the evenings and watched VHS tapes of recent movies, like a large family. He wasn't locked into his room at night – a big plus. And once every few weeks during the summer they got to go to the beach. "We'd go more often," a social worker explained to me one day, "but we can only take three or four at a time, and there are 18 in the house."

The next summer Sheila bought him a new swim suit and took him up to Charlotte's swim club a few times. Paul was quite a sight in that suit. He had huge, blue varicose veins rippling down his legs, and when he took off his shoes and socks, Sheila discovered his toenails were yellow and thick. While he was hospitalized, someone had supervised his cleanliness. But now he wasn't changing his socks and had developed a bad fungal infection. Sheila barraged the case workers with complaints for weeks before they took him to a podiatrist.

But if his hygiene suffered in this new setting, on the

general activity level it was a promising time. And what difference did it really make if there were bleach holes in his jeans? He survived his unsightly toes. He didn't get any better, really, but he was no worse, and he seemed to be enjoying life a bit.

After years of every visit ending with him begging us to let him come home with us, he now waved goodbye with a smile on his face. He liked Haven House. He liked driving down to White Plains during the week. For the past 18 years he had often spent weeks at a time without even going outside; now he was out every day.

Seasons changed, holidays came and went. No begging to come home with us, more laughter. The explosions and references to his hundreds of children and FBI work popped up from time to time. We had to be careful to hide alcohol from him if we had him home; his idea of a drink was to down an entire bottle. But he could also suggest different places to eat now and he knew the way to the nearest movie theater. He developed a little swagger to his step. Maybe it was better than the prison-like hospitals, after all. Maybe this out-of-hospital thing could work.

And then, one day, Patrick arrived to visit him and found, again, that Paul wasn't there. He and his roommate Marty had been moved to a "supervised apartment." After all, Mike explained, they had been teaching the men life skills for several years now. It was time for them to move on.

14. Bond, James Bond

Before Mother died, I had never second-guessed any of her decisions regarding Paul. The decision to commit him, the efforts to keep him in the hospital. I hadn't questioned the diagnoses of the doctors who had treated him. He was never going to get better and needed to be in a hospital. He could never take care of himself. And even worse, he might hurt someone.

He'd never be able to hold down any sort of job. And his hygiene was certainly terrible. Even with the rules at the halfway house, he sometimes arrived at family gatherings smelling so bad we had to send him to the shower. He went back wearing old clothes of my husband's a couple of times. Paul and Marty in their own apartment? A scary thought.

We were all afraid this move to an apartment would be a disaster.

"One of us visits him a couple of times a month!" Pat yelled on the phone to me as he explained what had happened. "Why can't they ever consult with us before moving him around?"

But the bottom line was that the state had a timetable and the social workers had followed it, without letting us know about it. Haven House was only a half-way house, half way between hospital and complete independence. The decision to give him more freedom seemed to be disconnected from any evaluation of his connection to reality. Unless he was a danger to himself or others, he was a free man. They had taught him how to cook and clean. Surely, we should be happy for him.

Of course Paul hadn't been hospitalized because he

didn't know how to boil water or set an alarm clock; he was in the mental hospital because he could not distinguish between his many delusions and reality. In addition, his repeated psychotic episodes seemed to have left him cognitively impaired. He didn't understand simple questions or cause and effect. He could not understand nutrition; he skipped meals or ate junk. Failure to eat regular meals changed the way his medications worked. If left to his own devices, he wouldn't take his medicine at all.

We imagined that he'd end up starting a fight with someone. What if he attacked some random guy in a bar? Would that guy talk him out of a confrontation, like Ken did? Or would there be bloodshed? How long before he was homeless, wandering the streets? What would happen to him then? What would Mother think?

While at the half-way house Paul had added another storyline to his FBI and Indian personas. Now he was also a millionaire movie star. He and a couple of his buddies had been in a toy commercial when they were about ten years old - for real; a neighbor worked for a toy company and had recruited them for a commercial where they sat around playing with toys. We had teased him at the time that he would grow up to be a handsome movie star. And now, he had become Western outlaw lawman Clint Eastwood, at least when he wasn't being a famous movie spy. "Call me Bond, James Bond," he would say with a phony English accent and a raised eyebrow. "But not the Sean Connery Bond, I'm the Roger Moore Bond."

"When I get out of here and get my millions, I'll buy you a big house," he told Ilene when she visited. (At my house one afternoon, when my husband complimented him for his work in *Dirty Harry*, Paul said, "Oh, that wasn't me. I was in *Hang 'Em High*.")

He couldn't make change for a dollar. He gave away a brand new Green Bay Packers sweatshirt, a present from Ilene, for two cigarettes. His clothes were alternately shredded or filthy. But according to the New York State schedule, it was time for him to transition to an apartment, so he transitioned.

As I drove to his apartment the first time, I tried to imagine treating another kind of neurological disorder this way. Tell someone with a spinal cord injury that they've been in a wheelchair long enough. *Time for you to walk!* someone says, and the wheelchair is whisked away.

Or imagine telling someone who suffers from Alzheimer's, *enough of this hanging around doing nothing. You've been in this nursing home for six months now. We can't look after you forever. From now on you'll have to take care of yourself.*

Absurd.

But Paul now lived in an apartment. We'd have to deal with it.

***

I have to admit that Paul was happy in that apartment.

It was a small, one bedroom unit on the ground floor, with a door directly to the outside, part of a large complex of long, low, two-story buildings in Elmsford, a town next door to White Plains, our old home. Each building had a row of eight or ten doors at ground level and a long narrow balcony with a parallel row of doors for the upstairs units. It reminded me of an older motel along a highway. New York State contracted with the Search for Change organization to manage several apartments in the complex. Three up and down units had been combined to make a half-way facility a few doors down from Paul and Marty, where staff were on call 24/7.

My very first visit I drove up and found Paul sitting outside with Marty, on a mismatched pair of rickety-looking lawn chairs. Paul was smoking a cigarette and drinking cold instant coffee. An old coffee can full of sand and cigarette butts sat on the ground by his feet. Both men were grinning from ear to ear. "Kathy!" Paul said, "You came!"

113

They showed me every inch of their small place. I had to sit on their couch and flick lights on and off in the bathroom. We opened and closed dresser drawers and kitchen cupboards.

"Can I fix you a coffee?" Paul asked. I accepted, although I insisted that he use water heated in their microwave, not lukewarm from the tap.

I had never met Marty before, but Sheila had told me about him, and Paul talked about him all the time. The two had been roommates for most of Paul's time at Harlem Valley, Hudson River, and Haven House. He was a soft spoken Black man, a little taller than Paul and a good fifty pounds overweight and a few years younger than my brother. He smiled a lot and seemed very calm. I was never sure what kind of mental illness he suffered from; he seemed more in touch than Paul. Privacy rules prevented the staff from telling us. All we knew was that the two got along great.

"Could you buy us a TV?" Paul asked as I was leaving.

"Sure," I said. And we gave him a VHS tape player and a bunch of Clint Eastwood and James Bond tapes for Christmas.

***

Paul was going on 40. I took him to an outdoor flea market/antiques show one sunny day on the Valhalla Dam plaza, not far from Paul's apartment. Paul was eager to wander around on his own. I watched him act the authoritative collector with one vendor and play quiet listener with a vendor anxious to show off his knowledge of different types of glassware. I giggled watching them.

At the end of one row was a booth run by a greyhound rescue organization. A large grey male greyhound wearing a service-dog vest rested in the shade of their table. Paul sat down cross-legged directly in front of the dog and began talking with it. One of the rescue volunteers and I watched Paul and the dog for a while.

"We take the dog to nursing homes. He's good with the

old people," the man said.

"Do you ever take him to mental hospitals?" I asked. "Looks like he'd be good at that, as well." I told him about Search for Change and he said he'd contact them.

"It's Charlie," Paul said when he noticed me looking at him. He petted the dog and looked into his eyes. "Charlie's in there. Look into his eyes. He found me."

The years in that apartment were Paul's glory days. He and Marty, hanging out, enjoying the fresh air. On their own, no locked doors, no one telling them when to go to bed or what to eat. Mornings, a van picked them up and took them to out-patient services in downtown White Plains, like it had when they were still at Haven House, only now the trip to the clinic was 15 minutes instead of an hour. Paul skipped most of the group sessions, though. Mostly he wandered up and down nearby streets smoking cigarettes and making faces at passers-by. My hairdresser, Karen, who worked at a salon nearby sometimes saw him strolling by and offered him a cup of coffee. She'd call me and report the sighting.

A few months after moving to the apartment, Paul and Marty began changing. We wondered if they were skipping their doses of Haldol or Risperdal or Lamictal or Clozaril or Thorazine (I'd lost track of what Paul was taking.)

We brought them to Thanksgiving dinner at Monica's house in her tidy Connecticut suburb, with its Laura Ashley wallpaper and floral upholstered love seats in the living room and plush corduroy couches by a big-screen TV in the den. Paul and Marty sat Indian style the entire afternoon in the middle of the living room floor, reeking of BO and mumbling incoherently. We brought them food to eat and coffee to try to wake them out of wherever they were. A couple of the men took them for a walk up and down the block. Sheila and her husband left early and drove them back to their apartment. They were upsetting the younger children.

115

At Christmas Paul was equally out of touch. When Sheila arrived to pick Paul up, she found that Marty had gone out with his own family. Paul was sitting alone and smelled pretty bad. She made him take a shower and change his clothes before she brought him to dinner.

***

It was a beautiful, warm Saturday the next summer. Sheila was away and had asked me to make sure I checked on him. I thought Paul would enjoy relaxing outside. I found him home alone, sitting in his apartment doing nothing. He limped when he got up to say hello. "It's that leg I broke playing football," he said. "It's killing me."

"You never broke your leg playing football," I said, which made him angry. I asked him where Marty was, and he started babbling, a sure sign something was wrong.

He was unusually quiet on the ride up to my house, and when we got home, I found a note from my husband saying he had gone out on a friend's boat for the afternoon. Paul and I were alone.

I started the kettle to make him some coffee, first thing. He was completely out of food at his apartment, and I figured he was both hungry and in caffeine withdrawal. As I opened the fridge to get out some cold cuts, I noticed Paul staring at me. He was doing his X-ray eyes thing, examining my breasts.

"Paul, quit staring at me," I said. I was in a loose fitting tee shirt, nothing suggestive.

He furrowed his eyes and stared harder, mumbling something.

"Why don't you go ahead out on the deck and have a smoke?" I suggested.

He considered that, but growled.

"Go on. I'll bring out the coffee and sandwiches when they're ready," I urged.

He tipped his head back, jutted his chin forward and

116

looked down his nose at me, like a wolf peering down along his snout. I stared back till he broke his gaze and wandered outside, where he sat at the table, watching the woods.

A conservation easement ran behind our house, and chipmunks ran and chattered beneath the bird feeder. The oaks and maples rustled in a breeze, and squirrels hopped and scolded. I breathed in and out slowly, then began to fix lunch. He sat very quietly outside, tendrils of smoke rising from his hand. I brought sandwiches and coffee outside.

"Charlie would have liked it here, don't you think?" I asked.

This brought a smile. "Sometimes when Pat takes me to his house I throw sticks for Rowdy," Paul said. "That dog! He's really Charlie, you know. I look into his eyes, and he winks at me."

We sat and watched the chipmunks at the bird feeder while we ate. Paul gobbled one sandwich and started on another. A cardinal was calling from a tree nearby, chirping and scolding. I didn't want to go back in the house with him.

"Wait here," I said and went inside and called my stepson and daughter-in-law. They were home with their eight-month-old infant, Alex. Kenny was a tall, strong young man, and besides, Paul acted very differently in groups.

"I have Paul home with me and he's being a little difficult," I said. "But I hate to take him back so soon. I thought he might do better around a few more people. Can we come by?"

"Sure," Jennifer said. "Come on over."

Their house was a short drive from mine, a pretty ride, past horse farms and a stretch of the Croton Reservoir. Paul liked riding in the car, and he was feeling better with some food in him. He'd eaten two sandwiches, chips, cookies, and downed a couple of coffees. He gazed out the window, quiet and smiling and watched fishermen out on their little aluminum row boats.

We sat out in the dappled shade of Kenny and Jen's deck, and Jen let Paul hold the baby, my grandson.

Alex Dering, 6 mos. old

"He's very smart," Paul said, after staring at him for a while. He cocked his head this way and that, examining him with one eye then the other, like a parrot, and spoke to him in gibberish for a few minutes. The baby gurgled back. Paul laughed. "He's a wise, little old man. I can't believe how smart he is! He says he's glad I'm here." His laugh went into a cough, and I took the baby.

"You gotta quit smoking!" I said for the hundredth time.

"I know, I know," he wheezed.

We hung around for an hour or so, then stopped at a grocery store on the way home. I bought him and Marty $100 worth of groceries, enough to last them a while, cans of franks and beans, frozen cooked chicken and pizza, a couple of gallons of milk, Cheerios, bread, peanut butter, bananas, a big jar of instant coffee, orange juice, some cookies. We stowed everything in his cupboards and fridge, and as I drove away Paul was settling into his lawn chair with some instant coffee. He smiled and waved as my car pulled out.

I felt uneasy. Did we need to check up on him twice a week to make sure he was eating? Should we be cooking for them? I could drop off lasagnas and chicken casseroles. We needed to do something different.

118

But I didn't want to be alone with him ever again.

***

It turned out they weren't just skipping the drugs they should have been taking, they weren't even eating. They had apparently opted instead for marijuana and hashish. Drug pushers knew when the men got their disability checks. Search for Change gave them only half of their SSDI money at a time, on the afternoon they ran a van to the grocery store. But the boys often skipped the ride. Judging by their empty cupboards, they likely swapped all their grocery money for a few joints.

The social workers were aware of the drug pushers and had alerted the police to try to get rid of them. But as far as forcing their charge to take his medications or to spend his money in the grocery store, "Your brother has a right to decide how to run his life," one of the case workers told me. "We try to convince them that taking their meds and eating properly is in their best interests, but our clients make their own choices."

Every time I saw Paul he was worse, more delusional, less in touch with reality. No matter how we scolded, he was deteriorating at an accelerated pace, both mentally and physically. All of us get older every year, but with Paul it wasn't a matter of a few wrinkles or thinning hair, it was like some mad genie had replaced the smart, handsome younger brother I once had with an old, bizarre, out-of-touch ringer.

I found myself avoiding visiting him, even with Sheila. It was so unpleasant, so upsetting.

My daughters were now both living in the City. Charlotte, my older girl, was in law school at Columbia; Loretta, my younger one, was finishing up at NYU. Ken and I both spent late hours at our jobs, I squeezed in some time working on a degree in creative writing at a nearby college, and on our vacations we began doing some travel – a cruise to Istanbul, another through the Panama Canal. I had a life.

I visited Paul with Sheila every few months but held out

119

little hope he'd get better.

It felt like we would go on this way indefinitely

In the fall of 2002, I got a call from Paul's psychiatrist. He'd suffered another psychotic episode and was back in the hospital.

15. The Consequences of Smoke

As I drove to White Plains Hospital the next morning, I wondered about what had prompted this break. It was fall, and the way the sun beamed down warm through the car windows on this crisp, golden day reminded me of the days of our mother's wake and funeral. I sometimes felt a tightness in my throat, an urge to curl up in a ball and think about eternity this time of year. Where do we go when we die? As much as the empiricist me was convinced that there was no afterlife, I was tempted to wonder if we might someday meet again. Could the crisp fall weather be a trigger for him, too?

I wondered at some unjust god, who would let him stumble through empty, meaningless days, a drain on our society, a heartbreak to our parents, a continuing worry to his remaining family, the butt of jeers by unfeeling neighbors and passers-by, often taunted by his many delusions. Why was he left here on this earth?

I'd given my telephone numbers to Paul's doctors and social workers for years, but no one had ever called me until the previous day.

"Yes, I'm his sister," I said to the polite-sounding woman's voice. "You called?"

It was a Doctor Becker, Paul's psychiatrist. Paul had been walking up and down Martine Avenue outside the clinic, menacing passers-by, accusing them of having stolen his ribs and punctured his lungs. "He believed he had been scalped and that he was bleeding profusely. Even when we stood him in front of a mirror so he could see that his hair was all still there, he could not be convinced that his head was intact. He insisted he had been scalped," she said.

The same delusion that precipitated everything, back in 1976. He hadn't been this bad in over twenty years.

I wasn't home back in 1976, that night Paul first came downstairs screaming about Indians, but Mother and the little kids told the story so many times, and I've told the story so many times, it's almost as if I was there.

I can hear 16-year old Paul thunder down the stairs in his heavy boots. He's always loved to wear big boots. I see him push aside the old glass pocket door and step into the dining room. Blood is trickling down his face and neck from all the razor nicks on his scalp. His hair – shoulder-length blond waves – is gone. His arms held high, wrists bent at an odd angle, fingers splayed, shoulders hunched, he's screaming, "I've been scalped! I've been scalped!"

My father looks up from his dinner, angry at first. Then something dawns on him. His mottled Irish skin turns purple. His blue eyes open wide, displaying the blood-shot whites. His bushy red eyebrows arch in dismay. For once, he is tongue-tied. He is frozen in his seat. Ilene and Julie are frozen in their seats.

"They're killing all the Indians!" Paul shouts. "Can't you see?" He looks around, then runs into the kitchen, and the back door slams.

They hear a car start. Paul doesn't have a driver's license yet, but he's been practicing driving the VW bug up and down our long gravel driveway.

Mother has been holding her fork an inch or two above her plate. It falls with a clatter. "John!" she says, leaping to her feet. "Stop him!"

Ilene and Julie start crying. "What's wrong with Paul?" one of them sobs. Everyone runs to the kitchen.

All that's left of Paul is a trail of red blood droplets, running all the way from the third floor bathroom, down the stairs, through the dining room, across the kitchen linoleum, and down the back steps.

It's too late! It's too late!

And now he was back to the same place. Same delusion. Another hospital.

As Paul got used to his freedom in his apartment, he loved doing things he hadn't been allowed to do at the hospitals, like walking around outside in the middle of the night.

Skinwalkers move in the shadows. When a skinwalker targets you, it generally comes at night.

Paul was ready for them.

Recognition Award

presented to

Paul Flannery

Lying out on the grass at about 2 a.m. one clear fall night, looking up at the stars for one of the first times in his adult life, he smelled smoke. He sniffed the air. It was coming from an apartment in his complex. A baby was crying inside, and he pounded on the door but got no answer. "Fire!" he yelled. He went around banging on apartment doors yelling, over and over. "Fire!" When the fire department arrived, he was insistent that they search for the baby. An eighteen month-old little girl was saved.

From that time on he had hardly been able to sleep, Dr. Becker said. The local paper carried a story with a picture of the jubilant mother hugging her rescued baby. The social workers at his treatment center had a little ceremony and gave him an award. But Paul was now a wreck.

Was she telling me he saved a baby and it caused a breakdown? It didn't compute.

All she knew, she told me, was that he kept screaming

that he'd been scalped. He'd been taken to White Plains Hospital "for his own good," she said.

I couldn't see him that afternoon, as he'd been heavily sedated. "They had to tranquilize him so that he can get some rest. He hasn't slept for days," she said, then gave me the phone number of the psychiatric ward and the name of the admitting physician. That evening I started the telephone chain.

It was Sheila who thought to call Marty. He and Paul didn't like being separated. Sheila's call found him in tears. He was such a soft-hearted guy. No one had informed him of Paul's hospitalization, and he'd been pacing their apartment for hours, wondering where he was. He was relieved that Paul was being cared for.

The next day, I went through two sets of locked doors to get back to the psychiatric ward at the hospital. Pleasant attendants asked if I'd brought any presents. They rummaged through my bags, confiscated the jar of decaffeinated instant coffee, and eyed my purse. "Anything glass, any knives, rope, metal implements?" I shook my head.

A male attendant in green, surgical-type garb unlocked a third door and ushered me through to an interior corridor. Bright afternoon sun streamed in through the day room windows. He pointed down a hallway. "Your brother's in room 8." I found Paul sleeping, huddled under a thin blanket and I shook him awake.

"Kathy! You came!" Groggy, he got up and hugged and kissed me, while trying to hold shut the pair of short blue hospital gowns – one tied in front, the other in the back– which barely covered his torso. No buttons, drawstrings or zippers allowed.

Paul's roommate was moaning in his bed, a pillow over his head. I ushered Paul into the hallway, where we sat in blue, hard plastic chairs just outside his room. I handed Paul a small, red, Metropolitan Museum of Art shopping bag filled with leftover Halloween candy that made it past the security check. He dug in with a grin and smacked his gums on the chocolate and sugar treats. A two-pack-a-day smoker and heavy coffee drinker, Paul had been denied both for over twenty-four hours.

I reached over and massaged his shoulder. "We're so proud of you, Paul. You did the right thing, calling the fire department."

"But what if I hadn't been there?" Paul asked me, his mouth full, bits of colored sugar falling from it as he spoke. He shook his head. "That baby would have died." He started to wheeze with imagined lung damage. He coughed, then leaned his elbows on his knees and held his forehead in his hands, shaking it back and forth, rocking on legs that would not be still.

"Paul, you're OK. You weren't in the fire, and no one was hurt."

He looked up at me, froze, and asked, "But what should I do about it?"

"Just be proud. Be happy. You did the right thing. You don't have to do anything else."

A short, middle-aged, Hispanic woman entered the floor, led by a nurse with a big ring of keys. The newcomer nodded at us as she was led into Paul's room to visit his roommate, the moaner, a young man barely into his twenties. He leapt out of bed when she touched his shoulder and rushed into the bathroom, stuck his head in the sink and ran water over it. The woman stepped out into the hall next to Paul and me and nodded toward the bathroom. "My son," she confided to us.

"My brother," I said. "*Mi hermano.*"

She was happy that I spoke some Spanish. "*Su cabeza.*" It's his head, she told me, tapping her forehead and nodding again toward the closed door. Her son thought water would cool it down and keep it from exploding, she told me in Spanish. She gripped and twisted the strap of her handbag, looked up and down the corridor.

I sensed that she was new to this.

Paul was eating package after package of Smarties, opening the cellophane packs two and three at a time and pouring the little candies into his mouth. They were spilling all over the floor and onto his blue slipper-socks with white rubber zig-zag treads. Above them, his legs looked sickly pale and were criss-crossed with ugly blue varicose veins.

And what…? She looked toward Paul.

"Eighth," he mumbled, his mouth full. She looked at me, quizzically.

Eighth of ten children, I told her in Spanish. He thought you were asking for his birth order. Usually when we tell people we are one of ten children, people want to know our birth order.

"Diez hijos! Imaginate! Y usted?" And you?

I'm second. I was twelve years old when he was born.

She pulled back her head with a start. "*El es el menor?*" He is younger than you? she asked. I first thought he was your father.

It's the illness. "*La enfermedad.*" He's only forty, but he has no teeth. He's been ill for more than twenty years.

And they cannot help him? "*Ay, ay, ay.*" She keened and looked toward the bathroom door. She sat up, straightened her dress and again wrung the strap of her purse.

I turned to Paul. "C'mon, Paul, let's walk."

We knocked on the locked, Plexiglas screen at the nurse's station. The window slid to one side, and we gave the nurse most of the candy to save for later. She wrote Paul's name and room number on the bag with a thick black marker.

Near the nurse's station, a young woman approached us. She had long, straight, light brown hair, a gray sweat suit and bounced from foot to foot, smiling winningly. "Please unlock the door for me; can you please unlock the door?" she asked me. "I have to get something that I left on the other side of the door."

She followed us, dancing on tiptoes. "Please? I just have to get to the other side of that door." An attendant hurried to her side.

We walked down a corridor past several closed doors. Paul pointed out the room where patients were tied down if they were too unruly. We stood and looked through the chicken wire-laced small window. Other than an examining table and some sort of cupboard, the room was empty and dark. "I've been in one of *those* before," he said, shaking his head slowly. "They zap you. You don't want to be in there. Believe me." He shuddered and we moved on. Had he been shocked? No one told me. I didn't want to ask him. I wouldn't be able to trust the answer, anyway.

At the end of the hall we turned around and headed back to our plastic chairs. I gave him the last three bags of Smarties from my purse and he ate them all at once; bits of sugar spilling from his lips. His hair was a wild, dirty tangle; I tried to tame it for him with the small brush from my purse. He winced with the pressure, but didn't fight me.

"Let's put together a list of things you need." I suggested as I brushed. "I'll ask Patrick to stop by your apartment and pick up some sweat pants, a comb, and some underwear and socks…"

"When I was in seventh grade, my hair was eleven inches long," he said. "It was black and very straight. I was an Indian then, you know. Me and Dickie and Homer were on the football team."

"C'mon, Paul. Let's not talk nonsense. You've always had blond hair. And football was over twenty years ago."

I tried to keep the conversation light. "Has Julie visited you lately? We told you, didn't we, that she and John had a baby? They named her Katherine."

Paul's eyebrows furrowed. "You know, us little kids are

important, too.   Wouldn't it be neat if we could just shift everything around? I'd be third and you'd be ninth. Julie would be oldest."

"But we can't. She isn't."

His smile disappeared. His lip curled. Simon Lagree. "She's evil, you know. She should never have had that baby. She just left it there. The whole place was full of smoke, and I could hear the baby crying, and I could see her and Homer and Dickie all running away..." He was shouting now.

Homer and Dickie and Paul.   A newspaper snapshot of the three of them on the seventh grade football team. Holding Paul in my arms to give him a bottle. He has beautiful blue eyes and silky blond hair, with lashes so long Grandma says he's too beautiful to be a boy. He's a cute four-year old, giggling with Julie and Ilene in the back of the gold '57 Plymouth station wagon when Mother picks me up after high school swimming practice. I come home from college and as I open the front door, a cute, tow-headed eight-year-old shouts, "Katherine's home. Katherine's home!" and runs into my arms.

"Paul, that wasn't Julie's baby. You're thinking of the baby you saved. And Homer and Dickie were nowhere near that fire. They're all grown up now and moved away."

His body relaxed. "Yeah. I guess," he said. He put his head in his hands again and sighed. "But what should I do about that? I mean, I just don't know what I'm supposed to do now."

"You should just be happy. Be glad you were there. That's all."

"Yeah.   Glad."   His face went through eight or ten different, contorted expressions.

"You know, I'm tired of being drugged up!" he suddenly shouted. "It's your fault, Kathy. I wouldn't be here if it weren't for you. You're the one who keeps telling them I have to be drugged up. There were five of them holding me down, trying to force drugs into me. But I have my rights. They shouldn't be able to force me. The police came and put me in here."

"Paul, you were walking up and down Martine Avenue screaming about being scalped. You were scaring people."

He shrugged. "Yeah. I guess I shouldn't do that." He started laughing and rapped,

"If you take a look at my mental condition,
and you multiply it by the economic situation,
it will lead you to the realization
that marijuana should be my medication.
... Just do the multiplication!"

He grinned, laughed, repeated it with variations.

After 45 minutes I was exhausted and I told Paul I had to leave to do some errands. It broke his trance and he thanked me for taking time out to visit him, then asked me to leave cigarette money with the nurse. "No cigarettes in here," I reminded him. He suddenly looked very tired and dropped his head into his hands. I took him back to his bed.

The nurses assured me that Paul received his medication that morning without any trouble.

"They had to take him off the medications he was on before," the nurse who was caring for him this shift told me. She was youngish with short, dark hair cut in a bob, a pleasant smile and a matter-of-fact way. "It's supposed to cause heart complications if taken too long. He hasn't adjusted to the new meds. It takes a while for them to build up in a person's system."

"Is that the real problem?" I was pissed. Doctor Becker hadn't said anything about changing his medications. "Was it the fire or was it the change in medications?"

The nurse didn't know about any fire.

I couldn't believe it. Couldn't the new meds have been phased in gradually or something? Was a heart attack any greater a risk than this? He was incoherent! They'd changed his medication, then denied him caffeine and cigarettes. I'd be off the wall, too!

129

"If nothing else, let him have a smoke, or give him a patch," I asked the nurse.

"Sorry. You'll have to take it up with his doctors. We can't give him a patch without a prescription."

I stomped a bit to let her know I wasn't happy. But I knew it wasn't this nurse's fault. She didn't decide which medication to give him. And the prescription change had happened before Paul even got here. She agreed to make a note on his chart about a nicotine patch.

The young woman who needed to get to the other side of the door had stationed herself in front of it, so the nurses let me out through the back of their workstation.

I made my way through the maze of locked doors and took a deep breath outside. As I walked to my car, I thought about a little baby who, fire fighters say, would no longer be with us, except for Paul's quick thinking. He saved a child's life. That must count for something.

Patrick stopped by the hospital the next day with a lightweight sweat suit and socks. Monica drove over from Trumbull, Connecticut to visit a couple of days later and brought more buttonless, zipperless clothes, as well as applesauce in non-glass containers and his favorite apple turnovers that he could eat without teeth. The social workers brought Marty by to visit, and the two old friends caught up.

Later in the week I called the hospital, intending to stop by on my way home from work, but Paul was no longer there. No one could tell me where he was. "I'm sorry, there is no one here by that name," was all anyone would tell me. I tried reaching Dr. Becker, but the clinic was closed for the day.

I left work as soon as I could and on a hunch drove to his apartment, where I found him sitting outside with Marty, drinking a big mug of instant coffee, smoking a cigarette and grinning from ear to ear. The coffee looked terrible. He'd dumped four or five spoonsful of instant into cold water – it was still floating on the surface. He wasn't making much sense, babbling on about fighting Indians and escaping fires. But he and Marty were deliriously happy he was home.

***

Now, when I drove Paul to and from Westledge and a chemo or radiation appointment, he often talked about how much fun he and Marty had back in their apartment. He forgot about Marty crying because he was afraid, and about their not having enough money for food. He forgot about wandering around the neighborhood knocking on people's doors at 3 a.m., bumming cigarettes, and about scaring teenage girls after school. What he remembered was sitting in the sun, smoking a cigarette and drinking his coffee, shooting the breeze with his friend. Isn't that what we all want?

It seemed a difficult goal for him to hold on to.

16. Transitioning

When Paul was moved to the apartment in 1998, people had told us he was no longer under hospital supervision, but we hadn't really understand what that meant. It appeared that he was being looked after by the people at Search for Change, so we continued to stop in haphazardly every month or so, like we did when he was still at Hudson River Psychiatric or at Haven House, his first post-hospital home. We saw Paul's breakdown and hospitalization as hiccups connected to switching meds, not a trend, and didn't realize how little direction he was being given until a downward spiral was already in full swing.

Sheila had been doing most of the visiting that winter and spring. It was a four-hour drive down from Boston though, so she only came once a month and she became concerned that Paul and Marty were both losing weight. Paul was making less sense, too. The doctors and social workers we spoke with didn't have any plan for new treatments that might help him improve. She asked me to check up on them in between her visits.

One Sunday I stopped by and found a stained mattress leaning against their lawn chairs in front of their entry way. Inside, I found Paul sitting alone on the couch doing nothing. The place reeked of urine. Marty wasn't around and Paul seemed confused.

I opened the windows wide and checked the kitchen cupboards. A couple of cans of pork 'n beans, nothing in the bread drawer, the refrigerator virtually empty. "C'mon," I said. Let's get you something to eat."

Search for Change maintained a halfway house a few doors down where they looked after a few recently released patients and maintained staff to help all their clients in apartments. Paul and Marty were supposed to go there every morning to take their medicine and any time they were having any problems. I took Paul over to ask the staff person on duty if they had Paul and Marty's food stamps. Paul had said they didn't get them anymore.

We walked in without knocking and found a few residents sitting in the living room on overstuffed brown couches like the one in Paul's apartment, watching cartoons. I could smell popcorn. The staff member on duty was a heavy set young woman named Monica. She had bright red fingernails about four inches long that curled like red snails under her finger tips, making them almost unusable. I wondered how she dressed herself. "Can you help us with Paul's food stamps?" I asked.

She took a last look at the cartoons on TV and sighed a deep sigh, shaking her head.

"They have no food. Paul has no money and Sheila says he has no food stamps," I explained. "Don't you take them grocery shopping every week?"

She pushed herself to her feet and huffed and puffed as she walked us over to a table in the kitchen, where she sat again with a loud "oof!" "The van goes to the grocery store on Wednesdays," she said. "If they're here, we take them. As far as food stamps go, in January a new system came in."

"Paul, we've told you this," she said to him, exasperated. *How many times do I have to tell him?* And to me, "There are no more actual stamps. They have to get a swipe card that is replenished electronically. I gave them their forms to fill in months ago. If they didn't fill them in, that's their problem. We can't do everything for them. They have to learn how to take care of themselves."

James Bond didn't fill out forms.

"Could you look up whether he took his medication

133

today?" I asked. "He seems a little off, even for him."

"Of course he took his medications," she said.

I tried not to sound pissed. "Could you check for me, to make sure?" I asked.

She sighed again, a long, exasperated sigh, got up slowly and walked over to a cupboard. Using the tips of her nails and the side of her hand, she managed to pull out a loose leaf notebook and rummaged through it. "He took his meds. As I told you," she said.

I thanked her for her trouble and wrote my address on a piece of paper. "Could you get copies of the food stamp forms and send them to me?" I asked. "Their money would go much further."

"That's not supposed to be our responsibility," she began, but paused when she saw my grimace. "Oh, all right. We can help them, I guess," she finally said with an exasperated sigh. "I'll leave a note for the Monday staff."

She picked up a pen using the tips of her two index fingers and began, laboriously, to write something down. I shook my head, and Paul and I left.

I bought him groceries with my own money.

I was so pissed. I don't know what bothered me more, the ridiculous notion that Paul could fill out his own forms, or her obvious indifference. This was her job, wasn't it? She was supposed to be helping Paul and Marty navigate living outside the institution. She acted like it was some big imposition on her free time.

The next week, I took an afternoon off from work to meet the social worker and psychologist assigned to his case. Julie and Monica joined me as well. It was to be a meeting to discuss Paul's future. We hoped we could all agree to get Paul moved somewhere he could have more supervision.

The mental health clinic that serviced Paul and Marty

was housed in a building that used to be a Sears tire center in downtown White Plains. I'd been there before. There were several small offices and a large day room for group meetings, as well as a conference room with a large wooden table and a dozen or so cushioned chairs. Clients milled about outside and in the day room. Paul joined us in the conference room.

He was happy to see us, and we talked about going out for a pizza when we were done. When the psychologist and social workers all started talking about some visits they had made with Paul to group homes in the area, though, his face fell. They turned to him every now and then but mostly spoke to me. And the more they talked the more agitated he looked.

Apparently Paul had gotten into arguments with people at both homes they had visited. The managers of two other group facilities that might have been appropriate for him had reviewed his case file and decided he would be too much trouble; there was no point in even visiting them. Bottom line? Not one of the homes would accept Paul.

I was confused. I looked at Monica and Julie. They seemed equally confused. Had the social workers already realized he couldn't make it on his own? Were they going to move him back into a more supervised place? If so, why were the homes refusing to take him? Wasn't that the job of a group home? To care for the mentally ill? Wouldn't their clients be likely to misbehave from time to time? I tried to follow.

"And was Marty along on these excursions?" I asked.

"Marty and Paul have achieved different levels of competence with life skills and will likely be assigned to different living quarters," the senior social worker explained.

Paul jumped to his feet. "You are not going to split up me and Marty," he said. "We stay together."

"You wouldn't want us to hold Marty back, would you Paul?" the social worker asked. "He can make it on his own. It's for the best."

With that, Paul started shouting and speaking in gibberish, a made-up language that sounded like a cross between fake Russian and fake French. He paced around the room, yelling and breaking into English from time to time to repeat that he and Marty were best friends and shouldn't be separated. "Friends stay together. We are not leaving our apartment," he kept saying in one form or another. Then back to the gibberish, waving his hands over the room like a magician casting a spell.

Finally an aide stepped forward. "Come with me, Paul," she said. "I'll see if one of the others will take him for a walk around the block," she called over her shoulder as she escorted him from the room.

"Hang around, Paul," I called after him. "After we talk, I'll take you out for dinner."

"This isn't working," we said to his team after he'd gone. I was shaking my head. "He's so upset. Do you have to split them up?"

But even as we protested the separation, part of me understood that if Marty could make it in an apartment but Paul needed to go back into a more institutional facility, they might be *right* to split them up. Paul needed more care, and in a more structured setting he wouldn't have to cook or do grocery shopping anymore. There would be someone to tell him to take his medication, and to keep him busy and connected to reality. Marty would enjoy freedom that Paul couldn't handle. We could take Paul to visit Marty. We'd make sure they stayed in touch.

The psychologist was nodding his head but the social worker was shaking hers. "We can't do everything for him, you know," she said. "It isn't our job to shop and cook for him. He could do it if he tried. He just has to pay attention. He has to learn how to take care of himself. We are being pressured to transition him. That's why he's acting up today."

"Transition?" we asked. "You mean go back to a hospital

136

setting?"

But no. We sat there dazed as they told us that Paul and Marty were in an apartment that was meant to be used for only one year. They had been there for over three years now, and it was time to *transition* them both somewhere else. *Transitioning* apparently only went one way. Out. The "homes" they were visiting were rooming houses, not mental health care facilities, and since none of them wanted Paul, he would be moved into a studio apartment where he would live by himself.

I felt like Alice in Wonderland.

"What are you saying?" I asked. "You know Paul. You saw what just happened. I thought we were talking about his need for *more* supervision. How can you be talking about a solo apartment for him? If he has to do it on his own, he'll have nothing to eat, he won't pay his rent, and the place will be a shambles. He'll be living on the street in a couple of months."

"The problem," they explained, speaking slowly and enunciating as if talking to two year olds, "is that Paul acts up whenever they take him to see a group home. There are very few places and they won't take him. They don't want a troublemaker."

"So you'll send him off on his own?" I could hardly talk. "At the very least, if there's no group home that will take him, don't split him and Marty up," we said. "They're good friends."

But there was no place in their system for good friends. They didn't seem to see either the illogic in releasing a man who was too troubled to make it in a group home, nor the cruelty of separating two men who had only a borderline grasp on reality.

"We've been charged with transitioning him fully into the community," they kept saying. "It's outside of our control."

"A place like Haven House," we took turns saying. "That's all he needs."

The logic got us nowhere. There were no supervised group homes. And the only way they could move him into a

137

hospital or more structured facility was if he became a danger to himself or others. They had decided he was not a danger. An hour of frustrating non-answers later, we left. Shaking my head, I looked around for Paul. Monica and Julie had to take off. I had planned to take Paul over to Nicky's, a pizza joint on Mamaroneck Avenue that we used to go to. He was gone, though. They had sent him back to his apartment in the van. He and Marty were safe for the time being. I was too tired to go see him and went home.

Mother had left a small trust for Paul that I looked after, but he would have burned through that money in less than a year, if we had used it to pay for his needs. Instead, we assumed the agencies were seeing to his basic needs, and we used Mother's money to buy him a TV and a few VHS tapes or new sneakers every now and then. We saved the rest for the day he would be released, cured.

Except for the extras we bought for him, Paul lived completely on Social Security Disability Income and Medicaid. Because Dad committed him before Paul's 18th birthday, Paul was treated as the minor child of a social security recipient and received SSDI every month. A large chunk of it was withheld by the agency assigned to him to pay for his housing, and the rest was meted out for him to use for groceries and personal items.

What we were having a hard time understanding was that the agency's role was drawing to an end. Since the time he had been discharged, back when they moved him into Haven House, the only reason he was being given any supervision at all was because he was in transition from the state mental hospital system. But this was only temporary. New York State had charged the agencies they had hired with moving *everyone* into housing for which the state had no responsibility. Now that the state had given the former patients self-sufficiency training, as far as New York was concerned, Paul and Marty were the same as any other residents of the state, responsible for taking care of

138

themselves. They were viewed the same as a malingerer or welfare cheat who wouldn't get a job. The social workers had found a rooming house that would take Marty in as a boarder and planned to find a studio apartment for Paul, at which point they could wash their hands of both of them. Paul, like Marty, would have to pay his own rent and manage his grocery money by himself.

The telephones buzzed again that evening, as the siblings discussed the day. It looked like we would have to play a larger role in finding Paul a secure place to live. We *had* to find a way to get him into an appropriate group home. Julia was working for a social services agency in Poughkeepsie, forty miles north of White Plains. She said she'd look into possible facilities near her.

A few days later, while Sheila and I were still discussing whom to complain to, the matter was resolved.

It seems that a couple of days after the disastrous meeting, Paul asked a thirteen-year-old girl in his apartment complex if she'd like to go to his place and watch a movie. She told her father, he complained, and in a matter of hours Paul was sent to Westchester Medical Center's psychiatric unit.

I found Paul pacing, yelling, furious at being put back in the hospital. True, he was slipping in and out of reality from minute to minute - his friends Homer and Johnny talking to him, playing football, hiking through woods with Native Americans, but he was not any worse than he had been for the last few years. He couldn't figure out why his world had been turned upside down.

"I just want to go back to my apartment," he kept saying. He didn't understand what he had done to justify being put back in the hospital. Neither could I. Because he talked with a girl in the apartment complex? I asked him about the girl, but he denied talking to any little girl, and if he had, he didn't see what

139

the big deal would be. He was still sixteen in some part of his brain. What difference could it make if he talked with some girl? I was happy, of course, that whoever the little girl was, she wasn't hurt. And I thought Paul *did* need some attention. He'd been looking worse and worse. I was sure he'd been skipping his meds, and he'd lost so much weight.

But why did someone else have to be in jeopardy for Paul to be given more intensive care? [5] And why did it have to be a locked ward again? Where were the supervised group homes that were supposed to be built when they closed the hospitals? If there were enough of them, there would have been no issue. A trained social worker would have been able to figure out that Paul was only argumentative because he was nervous about being moved, or might have recognized that his meds were off. But in the absence of the smaller facilities that hadn't been built, there was nothing between a large hospital, reserved for crises only, and independent living.

Doctors at the Medical Center could find no records on Paul's past psychiatric care. I asked Paul's social worker to get the White Plains clinic to send over their records, but the clinic had no information on Paul from prior to three years before, when he had been moved to the apartment. Haven House had been closed. No one knew where those files were. Westchester Medical Center personnel assumed he had been committed because of a psychiatric crisis and began testing various regimens again: Haldol, Risperdal, Lamictal, Clozaril, Thorazine... As one drug wore off and another hadn't reached

---

[5] As New York State commitment laws were written, a person with mental illness couldn't be forced into a hospital if they were not taking care of themselves, but only if they presented a danger to others. I liken it to helping a person with epilepsy only so that they won't have a fit in a public place and scare children. What about the person with epilepsy? More to the point, because people cannot be committed against their will unless they are a serious danger to others, the state no longer provided benign long term care facilities for people like Paul.

its full dosage, Paul was back into deep delusions, unable to engage in even his usual half-crazy conversations.

Six weeks later they sent him to Rockland Psychiatric Center, the same place he'd been committed to back in 1977. It had been more than twenty-five years of no progress. Marty was placed in a group home in nearby New Rochelle. We went to pick up Paul's things from his apartment, and except for a small box of pictures and a couple of video tapes which was being held in the office, Paul's things – his TV, most of his clothes, a few mementos – had disappeared.

17. Lost

Every time Paul moved, he lost things. Hats, coats, shoes, underwear, sweaters, bathing suits, books, letters, snow-globes, vhs tapes, birthday cards, TV sets, photographs. Even moving from one room or ward to another one at the same hospital, Paul's belongings seemed to disappear. I guess it's no surprise that social workers lost his files and medical staff lost his medical history. He'd obviously lost his mind. No surprise we lost *him* every once in a while. In the fourteen years between Mother's death and Paul's diagnosis with lung cancer, we lost him more than once. Because we didn't hang around and talk with the social workers as much as Mother did, we didn't find out he was being transferred from one hospital to another, or one building to another until after the move took place.

I tried to stop by after work to see Paul at Rockland Psychiatric Hospital once a month or so. The community bank where I worked was in Rockland County, only seven or eight miles from Paul's new home, so a visit was only a few minutes out of my way. There were many more buildings at the Rockland facility than there were at Hudson River or Harlem Valley. All the patients seemed to be concentrated in a couple of 1960's era towers. All around them, like abandoned slave shanties, rows of white, wood-shingled bungalows and small, two-story colonials stood empty, with windows boarded up and tall weeds growing through cracks in the sidewalks. They had been used as group homes, and patients were no longer housed indefinitely like the old days.

For the first few months, while he was under evaluation, Paul didn't have a grounds pass, so we couldn't take him out.

142

When I visited, we hung out in a visiting room on the first floor, near the first set of double locked doors. I stopped and picked up take-out from a Chinese place one night, and we chatted while he ate. There was another family visiting – a Hispanic woman, the patient's wife probably, and two children. Their dinner smelled great, some sort of spicy chicken and rice, I think. Paul and I sat at our own small square table and they sat at theirs. Each of us talked in hushed tones. Paul told me that he was cured now and he'd be out in no time.

"There's a good Paul and a bad Paul, that rascal," and the rascal was gone.

***

The bank where I was working once had an officers' planning luncheon at the country club a couple of miles down the road from Paul's hospital. The club house was on a small hill, and from the dining room windows you could see the World Trade Center Towers across the river in Manhattan.

The year before Paul was re-hospitalized, while he lay withdrawing from one medication and before readjusting to another on the upper floors of Building 32 at Rockland Psychiatric, the upper floors of those two tall towers across the Hudson collapsed in flame and rubble.

I was supposed to be up on the top floor of one of those towers that morning. I'd planned to attend a breakfast seminar for community bank treasurers and CFOs being held in the restaurant on the top floor, but I'd complained about it at dinner a few nights before. I was so busy at work, and I'd have to get up at about 5 am to make it all the way down to the foot of Manhattan for a breakfast meeting and then pick up my car and drive in to my office and work till ten pm to catch up. Ken had encouraged me to cancel, and I did. The people who attended that day all died.

Why was I one of the lucky ones in this life? Intelligence, education, opportunity, sanity, I'd been dealt a royal flush, while

143

Paul got a raw deal. What he would have done to have the opportunity to learn to fly a plane and the freedom to travel! The terrorists had everything and threw it away. The world seemed to make no sense at all.

Not long after returning to Rockland Psychiatric, Paul was admitted to the local medical hospital with pneumonia. I had called his ward before going to visit, or I would have gone to the wrong place. No one had notified any of us that he was ill.

He looked very old and scared, lying in the blue and white hospital gown, IV in his arm, his eyes closed. He was in a small single room; no cards or flowers – he'd had no visitors till now. He practically cried when he saw me. He'd been there for three days and couldn't tell me who his doctor was or what his treatment would be. His mojo was gone. He had enough wherewithal to ask me to give my credit card number for him to get TV service, which I did. But he was really out of touch. Football, fires, Indians, crying children. I had brought magazines for him to read, but he just flipped through the pages. I suspected he was becoming farsighted, so I got him some drug store reading glasses from the gift shop downstairs. He said they helped.

***

Sheila arrived at Rockland Psychiatric one day the summer of 2004 and again found he was not on his ward. He wasn't back in the hospital, either. "There is no one by that name at this facility," was all the woman at the front desk would tell her. Sheila finally got to speak by house phone to someone on Paul's old ward, who told her Paul had been moved to the experimental center.

"He volunteered for a clinical trial of a new medication," the aide said.

Paul had been asked to take part in experimental drug trials being conducted in another building in the complex. We found out later it was for Abilify, which was supposed to help anti-depressants relieve depression. Paul wasn't depressed, though. The testing was to see if the drug caused liver or kidney damage. He was a human guinea pig.

Sheila called me in tears from her cell phone as she drove across the huge hospital campus to the testing ward. "Volunteered? Don't you need to have a functioning brain to give informed consent?" Sheila ranted. "Did it occur to anyone to speak to the family? No. Of course not."

As we talked, I almost expected she'd find him in a cage. I pictured rows of men and women in ill-fitting, Goodwill wardrobes, crawling around behind metal bars, like the monkeys and hamsters I'd seen in movies about animal experimentation.

Thank goodness the experimental center was a newer, one-story building with big windows and pleasant rooms. No cages. The staff was friendly and happy to call Paul for her.

"Sheila! You found me!" he said, giving her a big hug and grinning from ear to ear. "Great place, eh?"

I stopped by to see him a few days later. He greeted me with a big smile. He was in a small unit, the building was sunny, and he got more personal attention here than he did in the tower he had been in. The patients and staff sent out for pizza or Chinese food on Friday nights and had a little party, watching rented movies together. One of the doctors actually asked to meet with family members to see if we could fill in more of Paul's medical history. The few records he could find from all the previous hospitals were a jumble. Little by little, he put together a more complete picture of Paul's past and along the way managed to balance his medications.

I complemented the doctor on Paul's improvement and asked if it was a new therapy. "No," he said. "We just got the meds tuned up a little."

Within a couple of months, Paul was better than we had seen him since he was first at Haven House, four or five years before. When I picked him up for a visit, he seemed a little more connected to reality and calmer. He started fewer arguments. As I sat with him at a nearby McDonald's six months later, I actually found myself asking him if he thought he'd like to get a job in a McDonald's one day. He still talked about scalping and his life as Clint Eastwood every now and then, but there were long minutes of lucidity.

And then, as abruptly as it started, the drug trial ended. State law and Medicaid would allow the hospital to keep him no longer, so all the psychological help came to a sudden stop as well. Three years after he had spoken to the 13 year old girl, the hospital packed up his few belongings in brown grocery store bags and released him to an adult home, called Hedgewood, in Beacon, New York, about midway between Peekskill and Poughkeepsie.

A five-story, cement-block building, from a distance Hedgewood looked a little like a dorm on a college campus. But nearby you noticed the obviously out-of-touch men wandering around town aimlessly or congregating in parking lots smoking cigarettes and shooting the breeze. Women paced around the parking lot carrying empty purses and wearing make-up that looked like it was put on without a mirror. They clustered around visitors begging for money and cigarettes.

Inside, the first floor didn't look too bad. There were red and white check tablecloths in the dining room, and little vases of plastic flowers. We were shown the nurse's office in the lower level. The place was staffed, however, with "dispensing agents," not nurses. A nursing staff would have caused Hedgewood to be designated an IMD, and they would have lost the right to accept Federal funding. They didn't dispense too well, apparently. Over time, as Paul had breakdowns and cycled into the local hospital, staff told Ilene that the folks at

146

Hedgewood were "frequent flyers." When brought in for psychotic episodes, they were often found to have less than the proper levels of their medications in their bloodstream.

Upstairs at Hedgewood, we discovered, was also an issue. The halls and stairwells reeked of urine. There were fist fights in the hallways. Ilene arrived for a visit one day and found an almost nude woman lying on Paul's bare mattress in a puddle of urine, smiling enigmatically.

A police car was often at the door, blue and white roof light twirling and flashing. Someone was always breaking down or creating a bad enough ruckus to be hauled off to the hospital or jail.

> *Hospitalization, stabilization, release, decline,*
> *No day clinic, no psychiatric care. You're in charge*
> *of yourself. Take your meds; you'll be fine.*
> *Psychosis, fights, rehospitalization or jail.*

> *Hospitalization, stabilization, release, decline*
> *Nothing to do and no supervision.*
> *Let someone know if an episode's coming.*
> *Psychosis, fights, rehospitalization or jail.*

> *One crowded building, 200 men and women,*
> *Delusions, mania, confusion, despair.*
> *Somebody crashes, now there's another.*
> *Police car stops. They're off with my brother.*

> *Hospitalization, stabilization, release, decline,*
> *Psychosis, fights, rehospitalization or jail.*

Because people with severe brain disorders in the US, like schizophrenia and bipolar disorder, are denied access to appropriate care, 200,000 of them are homeless, 300,000 of them are in prison, and they cycle in and out of the emergency rooms, psych wards, and jails by the millions. They die, on average, 25 years sooner than the average not-mentally ill person. Our society has decided they should just try harder. As if they had a choice. They end up, Murphy's Law style, in the least restrictive housing possible, where they are almost guaranteed to self-destruct. New laws, supposedly meant to protect their civil liberties, make it almost impossible to commit people against their will. Instead, they now face homelessness, incarceration, and death.

I hated going into Hedgewood. If it was my turn to take him out, I would ask someone to go upstairs and find him for me. One day, watching Paul come out to greet me in his saggy jeans, cigarette in hand, dirt and food stains all over his sweat shirt, I suddenly remembered how handsome he was before he lost his teeth, the way he bounced or swaggered when he walked, before he shuffled, before he lost his breath walking more than a block or two. Where had he gone, that 13-year-old with the shy smile, so proud of his football prowess?

As bad as I felt, though, tears welling up in my eyes, how must it have been for him? He remembered living at home with all of us in White Plains. He could describe his friends and their various childhood escapades as though they had happened a month ago, instead of decades ago. He was stuck there, mentally, his childhood buddies running through his imagination as though they were here with him all the time. But those friends had all grown up and moved away. Most had married and had jobs and families. How could he live with the depths that his life had become?

I didn't see too much of Hedgewood, luckily. Ilene had moved east the year before and was excited to finally be helping with Paul's care. "Okay, I'm here now," she announced to us all. "You've all been bearing the burden. Now it's my turn."

I was happy to be off the hook, and Sheila cut back on the long drives. She had spun out one rainy evening and was

148

getting nervous about driving so far, often after dark during the winter months.

Charlotte and Julie, who lived closer to Beacon than I did, took up the back-up visiting job. The younger ones remembered Paul as a teenager; they'd all been part of the little kid five. They took him bowling and to the movies, for meals at the diner or a Chinese restaurant. They walked down by the river or brought him to Charlotte's pool club during the summer. He had some good days, but more and more bad days.

We bought him Clint Eastwood tapes and a small TV for Christmas, but they broke or disappeared within a few months. Paul made a few trips to the hospital, to "rebalance" his medications a couple of times and twice for pneumonia. Ilene was the contact person now. She got the phone calls or noticed when he suddenly wasn't there.

A psychiatric nurse I know who works in a county hospital upstate told me once that they saw the same mentally ill patients cycle onto their ward over and over again. "It's David again," they'd say to each other when the call came in that a psychotic man had been brought into the ER. Or Cheryl, or John. They knew what drugs worked the last time, so they'd get him or her stabilized in four or five days, then release them to a taxi with a prescription they would likely never fill, $25 and one night prepaid in a local motel. They would be back in a month or two.

Ilene was determined to find someone who could help break the cycle, help Paul improve.

18. A turn of events

From: Ilene Flannery
To: Patrick Flannery, Katherine Dering, Sheila Flannery, Charlotte Flannery, Grace Flannery, John Flannery, Laurie Flannery, Monica Flannery, Julia Flannery
Date: Friday, April 06, 2007 10:49 AM
Subject: Re: Friends Adult Home

For those of you who hadn't been in on the past few days' discussions, I accidentally found out about a smaller Adult Home for Paul. It's a very old, large home (see the link below for the location). It is not the most beautiful place, but it was very clean and didn't smell bad. All of the bedrooms have hardwood, painted, floors with real twin beds with headboards and old-fashioned dressers - just like a real bedroom.

There are three, unoccupied bedrooms on the second floor and three bathrooms. They are also talking about getting a pool table! The woman who runs the place seemed very nice. She's been doing this for 18 years. All of the residents go to a day program in Rhinebeck where they do arts and crafts, painting, cooking, etc. It had a nice, homey atmosphere, which would be a great change from Hedgewood. They also have voluntary evening and weekend programs where they take them bowling, to the movies, etc.

The cost is $1500 a month and Josie said he'd need another $100 a month for incidentals - cigarettes and other spending money - they buy the cigarettes in bulk and then dole out - saves lots of money that way and they can control it. Social Security Disability Income will pay some, but we'd have to supplement from Paul's account to pay the rest so we'd have to decide if we are willing to take the risk that he would have run out of money in a dozen years or so. Quality of life now vs. running out of money when he's 60. I vote quality of life now.

Anyway, it's a first step towards what many of us had been discussing for the past year or so - wanting Paul out of Hedgewood. Sheila saw Paul yesterday - he's fairly agitated - I've possibly been seeing him too much - been "telling him what to do" too much - I'd gladly let Sheila be the boss and just be the sister who visits. So, we have to work out that dynamic and get him settled down again before springing this on him. I assume others will want to see the place and then Josie would want to see Paul before any commitment is made.

Let me know what you think.

Love, Ilene

P.S., did you see the name of the lake behind the house? If not, check out the map again. It's Lake Geneva. Can you believe it? It must be a sign.

From: Katherine Dering,
To: Patrick Flannery, Ilene Wells, Sheila Flannery, Charlotte Flannery, Grace Flannery, John Flannery, Laurie Flannery, Monica Leggett, Julia Brower
Date: Friday, April 06, 2007 11:18 AM
Subject: Re: Friends Adult Home
Paul's savings.xls (21KB)

The money Mother left in trust for him is not really very much, just enough for a few treats now and then and possibly some furniture if he ever gets better, and then to pay for his funeral. Attached is an excel sheet with

151

three variables - assumed return on the trust's portfolio, monthly shortfall to start, and, with an assumed inflation rate, showing increases in monthly shortfall eating into the corpus of the trust.

Assuming we use a few hundred a month, his money lasts almost into his sixties. When he's over 62, he can go into a nursing home, anyway, and nursing homes are fully paid by Medicare and Medicaid, etc. I'd say that if the place is decent, and if they are up to the task, why not give them a try?

We all remember what happened at the apartment, the last time Paul started on a downward spiral like the one he seems to be on.

From: Ilene Wells
To: Patrick Flannery, Katherine Dering, Ilene Wells, Sheila Flannery, Charlotte Flannery, Grace Flannery, Laurie Flannery, Monica Leggett, Julia Brower
Date: Tuesday, April 24, 2007 4:34 PM
Subject: Paul is at St. Francis

Paul was admitted to the hospital yesterday afternoon and it looks like he'll be there quite a while. I thought it was for psychiatric issues but when Sue - the nurse at Hedgewood Home - called me, she said he has Pneumonia again! It gets worse though...when I called St. Francis, they said he is in an isolation ward because they think he has TB! If we go see him we have to get all suited up. I am going over there tonight and I'll let you know how he is doing. Millie, the nurse at St. Francis, said he is comfortable and watching TV. He is in Ward "6-Cook".

They said he is being very cooperative and the psychiatrist saw him and his Schizophrenia is "under control" whatever that means. It will take them a while

> to get the tests back. Millie said he'd be there at least a
> month.
>
>> I am totally blown away.

When Ilene and Willy left their home in Wisconsin and moved east she thought she could be closer to Paul. They bought a little house up in Saugerties, Ilene imagining that Paul would get better one day, that he could come and stay weekends. But Paul got sicker, not better. Shortly before he was hospitalized this time, he told Ilene that he had come to the realization that he must fast from all food in order to find salvation. He'd lost 30 pounds in three months.

When it was time for him to be released from the hospital, Ilene and Julia insisted to the social workers that he not be returned to the adult home. He'd never give himself the nebulizer treatments he needed. After some effort, he was moved, instead, to Westledge nursing facility.

> **From:** Katherine Dering
> **To:** Ilene Flannery; Patrick Flannery; Monica Leggett, more
> **Sent:** Monday, July 16, 2007 7:00 PM
> **Subject:** Paul
> Att: westlletter.doc
>
> Ken and I visited Paul at Westledge today and talked with the social worker, Sharon. I know Ilene and Julie have been looking for a permanent place for Paul. But we've all been noticing that Paul is so much happier now, compared to Hedgewood. So I asked if they can keep him here.
> We thought once his pneumonia cleared up, he had to be released. The social worker said they can keep him there indefinitely, but cautioned that the State might give them a hard time, because the place isn't "appropriate" for him (it's really an old folks' nursing

153

home). A letter or two from the family saying we're happy with the situation and why, would be good to have in the files.

On 7/16/2007 Patrick Flannery wrote:

Katherine,
  I am ashamed of my ignorance on Paul's situation and condition, but I'm sure your assessment is good and you can add my name to the list of endorsees to your petition if you'd like. I wish I could be of more help.

Pat

From: Katherine Dering
To: Patrick Flannery
Date: Tuesday, July 17, 2007 1:51 PM
Subject: Re: Paul

  Actually, there is something you could do.
  Ilene is writing to Hedgewood to ask them to box up Paul's things.
  I, frankly, am sort of afraid to go into Hedgewood. The men who hang around in there give me the creeps. If you could pick up his things - mostly clothes, some pictures and a few things from his dresser top - I think the TV got busted somehow and the tapes all disappeared - that would help. I can pick them up from your house, and sort through them. (Call them first and see if it is ready - I'd give them a week.)
  And don't be ashamed. We all phase in and out of his life. I haven't done much for him lately, either. But it is really so much easier and more pleasant to visit with him in such a nice nursing home, no wackos hanging around, no cigarettes. It's so close, too - rte. 35 to Bear Mtn. pkwy for about two minutes, off at Peekskill - I think the

2nd exit, left turn onto rte. 6, Main St, and then the nursing home is on the right after about 100 or 200 ft.
I have more time now, but as I said, Ilene and I both hate going into Hedgewood.

On 7/17/2007 Patrick Flannery wrote:
OK I can do that

July 16, 2007

Ms. Sharon Schaefer
Director of Resident Services
West Ledge Rehabilitation & Health Center
2000 E. Main Street
Peekskill, New York 10566

Dear Ms.Schaefer,

Thank you for meeting with my husband and me today.

To reiterate our discussion about my brother, Paul Flannery, the family--my sisters Ilene, Sheila and Monica and I--have all talked amongst ourselves lately about how happy and healthy Paul is looking these days. He is happier, saner, and more physically fit than he has been in twenty years. During the two years or so that he was at Hedgewood, he had a couple of hospitalizations for pneumonia, the direct result of poor nutrition and smoking exacerbating his emphysema. He also was committed a couple of times to the local psych ward because he became psychotic. Tests showed that he did not have the proper dosage of his medication in his system- at the adult home they did not make sure he took it regularly. We also suspect he was not eating properly. By the time he was hospitalized most recently for pneumonia, he had lost over thirty pounds, and was really looking bad.
Paul suffers from pulmonary disease. At Hedgewood, they allow Paul to smoke. At West Ledge, you are able to keep him from smoking, and as a result he is much healthier. Also, whether

155

because of poor dental hygiene due to his mental problems or because of the dry mouth that was a side effect of all his medications, over the years his teeth were all pulled. At Hedgewood, they do not accommodate his need for more easily chewed food, and he sometimes cannot eat the meal they prepare. (He has twice been fitted for false teeth, but he won't wear them.) Also, probably because he never "grew up" outside an institution, he is very naïve and frequently gets taken advantage of. At the adult home, most of his clothes disappeared, as if anyone liked his sweatshirt or sweater, he would give it away, or trade it for one cigarette or a cup of coffee. After several months at West Ledge, he still seems to have his clothes and personal items.

Paul likes it at West Ledge, and although it may seem odd for a 48-year-old man to be housed in a facility where most of the residents are over 75, he is perfectly fine with it. He likes everyone there, the nurses, the aides, and seems content to be limited to the facility. And we, his family, are just as happy with the limitations.

So I hope he can stay with you for the foreseeable future. My sisters and I will keep looking for a smaller, "homier" place for him, some place where the other residents are closer to him in age and where they will be able to give him the supervision and structure he needs. But in the meantime, we are happy with him there, in your care.

On behalf of myself and my brothers and sisters, thanks for taking such good care of him.

Sincerely,

Katherine Dering

Once Paul became a permanent resident at Westledge, the staff doctor did a full review of his medical records. A tumor had been noted on Paul's lung, but it had gone untested through two separate hospital stays. The conscientious doctor asked, what is that shadow that I still see on this man's lung?

The biopsy results were bad. An oncologist was called.

The long hard journey began.

That fall, Monica and I took turns taking Paul to and picking him up from whatever doctors said would save him. Sheila, Patrick, Ilene, Julia and Charlotte filled in, as needed.

Paul seemed genuinely happy. Nurse Jill, the floor supervisor, nicknamed him "The Governor" because he went around shaking peoples' hands all the time. "What? Is he running for office?" she asked, laughing. The nursing home was bright and clean, the nursing staff always smiling. How could he not improve here?

Through all the long delays getting chemo at the hospital or waiting for doctor visits, Paul was cheerful and, for him, cooperative with Monica and me. He didn't glare and start arguments. Johnny visited from North Carolina for a few days. Grace flew in every few weeks – and we almost never saw Grace – and Paul seemed to enjoy the attention. As the holidays approached, though, we all picked up on a sense of urgency, a panicky feeling that there would not be a good outcome for all this.

> **From** Ilene Wells,
> **To**: Grace Flannery, John flannery, Kerry flannery, Laurie flannery, Michael Flannery, Patrick Flannery, Sean flannery, Sheila Flannery, Monica Leggett, Ilene Wells, Julie Flannery...more
> **Date:** 12/2/2007 2:11:34 P.M.
> **Subject:** Christmas presents for Paul
>
> Hello All,
> I was out shopping today and found a gift set of all of the original Spiderman cartoons. Paul and I used to watch

Spiderman every Saturday and I thought that since they are only a half an hour long, it would be easy for him to watch - his attention span isn't very long. I also happened to find two cd's of the original Little Rascals shorts. Again, he and I spent our mornings before school and other times watching Little Rascals, we used to love those shows. I am going to give him those for something to watch while he is having his Chemo on Tuesday.

As far as other, similar, shows we used to watch, I think Paul would like to get the original Batman series - not the cartoon - the ones with Adam West, as well as the Green Hornet with Bruce Lee. He might also like to watch the original Wild, Wild West shows. That was another series we used to watch before he got sick.

I talked with Katherine today about getting Paul a portable game device like Game Boy. Wow - we would never have thought about getting him any of this if he were still at Hedgewood. We are so lucky he is at a place where we can trust his belongings won't get stolen.

For those of you who do not know, Paul will be undergoing weekly Chemo sessions - at a third of the strength - instead of once every three weeks at full strength. It is too much for him to get it at full strength with the radiation. Monica has worked with the case workers at West Ledge – again, thanks to them for their caring and support – and figured out that he is also eligible for Medicare and can actually have the chemo treatments at the doctor's office from now on. Thank goodness for that.

I am working from home most of next week and will be with Paul for Tuesday's chemo treatment and Katherine will take him from Radiation to Dr. Ayan's office for the Chemo. I will be with him for Wednesday and Thursday's radiation treatments. I am glad to be able to help out. Monica and Katherine have been doing so much so far! I am glad to be able to relieve them somewhat next week. Sheila took a turn last week as well.

The doctor warned Monica and Katherine that at about

this time, the chemo and radiation will really start to take its toll on Paul. He already has some trouble swallowing and that will get worse. He will also not be able to digest milk products well either. Something to remember when you visit him. We are also trying to cut out all sodas - and trying to give him more substantial calories. If he won't be able to eat well, we need to make sure that what he does eat is good for him.

Oh, another thing he would like are music cd's. His DVD player can also play cd's. He mentioned wanting Stevie Wonder to Monica. I'll talk to him about it on Tuesday and let you know.

Love to all,
Ilene

From: Grace Flannery
Date: Saturday, December 15, 2007, 2:20 PM
Subject: Re: Christmas presents for Paul

Hi everyone, I just ordered a DVD of the first season of Kung Fu (David Carradine, Grasshopper, etc.) I hope Paul doesn't already have this! If anyone knows that he DOES have it, please let me know! And, Katherine, I'm having the DVD sent to my name at your address.
Can't wait to see you all!
Love,
Grace

Grace Flannery, PCC, CPCC
LEADING SPIRIT
Coaching for Life, Leadership, and Relationship

Monica had three huge trays of cookies, fruit and nuts delivered to the three shifts of nursing staff at Westledge. The nursing home set up a tall Christmas tree in the entry foyer, and the staff of the third floor decorated all the clients' room doors. It had a homey, relaxed feel, not the tense, tinseled fakery of the psych wards. And certainly unlike the filth of the adult home. This place looked quite festive.

Grace had visited at Thanksgiving, but at the last minute work kept her from making it back in December. John flew in for Christmas, though. And the locals all made an effort to show up for the big day at my house. Ilene's boys, 20 now, made it to New York, too. Paul seemed tired, but enjoyed himself. He was hardly delusional. We took lots of pictures.

For the Christmas birthdays, our sister Charlotte outdid herself. She made a three dimensional, Christmas tree birthday cake. We joked it looked like a green volcano. Ilene and Paul sat next to each other at the kitchen table and we all gathered around. Someone lit the candles and we all sang the birthday song with raucous abandon. The twins posed by their cake and blew out seemingly hundreds of candles. Patrick and Johnny shared Dad's job of wiggling their eyebrows and singing like opera singers.

Paul looked good. He was thrilled to have Johnny with us. He followed him around all day. He'd made it this far. We all tried to ignore the nagging feeling of unease and expressed hope that he would make it through the rest of the treatments. Ilene was already planning where he could live once he got better.

19. A life

Radiation began in January. It was more time consuming than chemo.

Five days a week an ambulette picked Paul up at the nursing home. That January and February we had more snow than usual for the New York suburbs, but five days a week Monica or I took our turns driving over the snowy roads to meet Paul at Mahopac Radiation Oncology. We sometimes brought coffee and shared it with him while we waited. His treatments were scheduled for the first appointment of the day – less time in the waiting room with other patients, we suspected. We got to know the receptionist and office manager, traded tips on the Thursday *New York Times* crossword puzzle, and the secretary explained to me one day how to care for a Christmas cactus. Mine at home hadn't bloomed in years. Theirs looked gorgeous.

She laughed. "Benign neglect. They won't bloom unless you take care of them right," she explained. "They need cool, dark nights and not too much water."

After the treatment, Paul and I drove around looking for something to do. We wandered around the Wal-mart and the Salvation Army store. We discovered a new diner and a Dunkin Donuts with an easy parking lot. I learned he hated movies about wars or with a lot of violence. He was a Beatles fan, but there was a Vietnam War scene in *Across the Universe* and he said, "I can't watch this," and walked out. He loved cartoons.

One sunny day, the snow sparkling and the air clear, Paul wasn't very hungry, so we skipped the diner. I blasted the heat and put the top down on my Audi convertible, and Paul leaned back to let the sun hit his face. I gave him one of the sodas I had on the back seat. He looked 100 years old. I knew the shots he was getting were painful, and we'd been told the radiation would burn after a while. His face was covered with a red scaly rash and he reached up and scratched his white, peach fuzz scalp under his knit cap. He was so thin. He had no eyebrows.

I thought about all the years he lived in mental hospitals, when we were off on our own journeys and hardly ever visited him. When we did visit him. When I was afraid of him and he must have sensed it. All the locked wards and heartless orderlies and no dental care and too many cigarettes and days and days of nothing to do except pace, think crazy thoughts, and wish he could go home, wish he could figure out what happened and how to fix it. I mean, was he shot in the head, or what?

We stopped at a light and Paul turned to me, his toothless face crumpling into a grin like a Jack-o-lantern a week or two after Halloween. He had a far-away look on his face. I asked jauntily, "How's it going?" fearing yet another story about Indians or bullets in the brain or excreting tumors out his butt or ghostly children springing up from lost teeth.

Paul leaned back in the warm leather seat, took a sip of his soda, nodded to the Stevie Wonder playing on the radio and grinned. "Now this," he said, nodding for emphasis, "This is the life."

20. Testing

From: Monica Leggett

To: Sheila Flannery, Katherine Dering, Charlotte Flannery, Grace Flannery, Laurie Flannery, Patrick Flannery, Monica Leggett, Ilene Wells, Julia Brower, Loretta Pontillo, Charlotte Pontillo, Melissa Leggett, Shelly Flannery, Sean Flannery, Kerry Flannery, John Flannery, Russell Leggett, Meghan Mahoney, Lucy Lesperance,

Date: Friday, February 22, 2008 4:28 PM

Subject: Paul

Hi Guys,

Paul had his PET scan yesterday to see if the cancer is gone, but we don't have the results yet. We should know by Monday or Tuesday. We'll start a phone chain or something once we know the results.

I picked up Paul at the nursing home at 1pm for a 1:30 test. He had not been allowed to eat breakfast or lunch. They brought up a lunch tray by mistake and he told them he wasn't allowed to eat it. Miss Jill was quite proud of him!

He did great at the hospital and through the test but he was starving afterward- it was 3:15pm. I took him to the Chinese restaurant for a meal he always likes- Shrimp Egg Foo Yung. He inhaled most of it! He still is very thin. I'm not sure what we can do about it but whoever visits him should try to get more food into him! Anyone going this weekend?

A sad note, Paul's roommate John died the other night.

His daughter was so good to Paul. She really seemed to care. Paul seemed to take the news well.   Katherine went up Wednesday to see him, make sure he was OK, and supervise his move across the hall. We think that's a policy that they move people if a roommate dies. He's now across the hall with the bed by the window.

I brought a sympathy card to send to John's son and Paul wrote, "May there be room in Heaven for John. Best of luck, Paul." I added a note from the Flannery family.

On that note I will say, have a good weekend.

Monica

From: Monica Leggett
To: Sheila Flannery, Katherine Dering, Charlotte Flannery, Grace Flannery, Laurie Flannery, Patrick Flannery, Monica Leggett, Ilene Wells, Julia Brower, Loretta Pontillo, Charlotte Pontillo, Melissa Leggett, Shelly Flannery, Sean Flannery, Kerry Flannery, John Flannery, Russell Leggett, Meghan Mahoney, Lucy Lesperance,
Date: Tuesday, February 26, 2008 5:37 PM
Subject: Paul news
Hello Everyone,

I spoke to Dr. Ayan finally and I'm sad to say the news wasn't good. I hate to share this news through an email but I don't know how else to get to all of you with all the info.

Paul's PET scan showed that there is a new area of concern on the left side. It is small, 1.5 cm, and in the center of the lung. He doesn't feel it can be biopsied right now, too small, too far in the center, not easily reached. The PET scan assigns a value to the level of metabolic activity and Paul's is 6.8. Anything above 5 is significant. When you consider that this new area grew while Paul was getting chemo and radiation you have to consider that Paul has developed resistance to the chemo. (The radiation was localized to the old sites so it probably wouldn't have done anything on the left side.)

The old areas are better than they were. The original tumor is gone. The two lymph nodes are dying off. (The PET scan shows they are emitting a signal that they are dying).

Prognosis isn't good based on the new info. Dr. Ayan feels it is now Stage 4 due to the new probable nodule. He wants me to call him back on Friday, I guess to discuss treatment issues. He doesn't feel it would help to do chemo again right now. He isn't sure Paul's body will tolerate it. The fact that he's down to 169 with clothes and hasn't put weight back on after the chemo and radiation were done isn't a good sign.

There is a new kind of pill that's been approved to treat a certain form of non-small cell cancer. He's going to check back into Paul's biopsy and see if it's a possible treatment. It's not chemo. It works against a certain protein on the surface of the tumor. I'm not sure of all the info.

Dr. Ayan wants to repeat the PET scan in 2-3 months to see if the nodule grows and how much. Other than the pill and the scan, he didn't say anything else to do.

Katherine and I think we should wait to talk to Paul until after I speak to Ayan. again on Fri. I'm going to visit Paul tomorrow but won't mention the test results. I have to leave for a meeting now, busy till 8:30. I spoke to Katherine so if you want to talk, call her or wait till 8:30 to call me. I'll have my cell with me.

We have to think of what's best for Paul now. I just wish I knew what that was. Love,

Monica

From: Monica Leggett

To: Sheila Flannery, Katherine Dering, Charlotte Flannery, Grace Flannery, Laurie Flannery, Patrick Flannery, Monica Leggett, Ilene Wells, Julia Brower, Loretta Pontillo, Charlotte Pontillo, Melissa Leggett, Shelly Flannery, Sean Flannery, Kerry Flannery, John Flannery, Russell Leggett, Meghan Mahoney, Lucy Lesperance,

Date: Wednesday, February 27, 2008

RE: Paul news

Hi Everyone,

I spent several hours with Paul today, took him to the diner for lunch. We went shopping afterwards to buy him an electric razor. He liked the idea of no razor blades and he's had some trouble with eczema or some sort of rash on his face for a while. We got it charged, he couldn't wait to try it, and he did pretty well and his skin didn't look irritated. He was all congested and wanted to rest so I left about 2pm.

I went to Dr. Ayan's office after that. I only wanted to tell him that Paul seems very congested, but after an hour wait in the waiting room he brought me to his office and we talked about everything. If only I had had the emails with me!

He prescribed an antibiotic for Paul, a Z-pack. He said Paul's threshold to tolerate infection is low and we should treat him. I asked what was the chance that the "tumor" is really an infection- he said only 10%. 90% that it's a tumor.

He made a copy of the PET scan report for me and explained again that if a new tumor grew during treatment means his cancer must have developed a resistance or had one right from the start. It also would appear that the cancer spread through the lymph system or the blood stream, a very bad sign. He didn't feel 1st line drugs will help anymore. He said some doctors would want to continue heroics at this point to cure the

166

cancer but there's a very slim chance for that. Paul has squamous cell which is the most difficult to cure. He proceeded to list and explain all the 2nd line meds we could give Paul. The list of 4-5 drugs are much easier to administer than all-day chemo and they also tend to have a lot less side effects: Alimta, Navelbine, Grisplatin, Taxotere, and Gemzar.

They are considered more as maintenance not a cure. They might keep the tumor in check-not growing, but not cure. He's recommending the Alimta.

As for radiation- He would not recommend. Lung tissue doesn't tolerate radiation well and could cause serious damage to the tissue. No matter what, he would expect to do a repeat PET scan in 10 weeks. I told him that I was sure we all want to do something. He agreed. I believe we can start one of the med routines as soon as we want to. Paul will be on the antibiotic for 5 days, hopefully will improve.

Ilene suggested we try to have a meeting amongst ourselves over the weekend. Sat eve or Sunday? Or we can keep talking over the internet. I would like Johnny to be in on the phone call with Ayan. on Friday if possible. What's your work schedule Johnny? Can we talk after 9:30 tonight (I have another meeting in a few minutes) or talk tomorrow afternoon?

21. Stevie

Re: Paul news
Date: Thursday, February 28, 2008 5:05 PM
From: Katherine Dering
Hello, all.

I had lunch with Paul today. He was unenthusiastically pushing some food around his plate with his fork when I got to Westledge, and was happy to go out. He chose to go to the New City Diner, where he gobbled a huge hot open face roast beef sandwich, and of course, his usual coffee and Pepsi.

I got a conversation going around the PET results, and I told him that the cancer wasn't gone, and that it looked like he would have to have a different kind of chemo. He right away said the doctor was just trying to drum up business, that the cancer *was* gone. But after I coaxed him a bit, he eventually admitted maybe it was still there and growing. "But I AM getting better. I'm sure of it," he said.

So I called Johnny on my cell phone and Paul spoke with him. Again, Paul started out saying the cancer was gone, but eventually admitted that maybe it was still there. Then he asked Johnny to look at his x-rays and stuff and tell him what he thought. They also had some sort of discussion about dying. Paul said his roommate, John, died, and maybe he was going to die. After something John said, Paul said he wasn't afraid.

Then Paul had a big chocolate shake.

On the way back from lunch, he said about five times, "Ah! That hit the spot!"

On one of our sister Grace's visits from California the previous fall, she had given Paul a fake Navajo blanket and a necklace of piñon nut beads. Monica gave him a Stevie Wonder CD for Christmas. The necklace disappeared one day, but Paul sat on the blanket and played the CD over and over again.

"What's your favorite Stevie song?" I asked Paul as we were driving back to Westledge. His Stevie was playing on the car CD player. He snapped his fingers and bopped his head and shoulders. "For once in my life I have someone who needs me..." he sang, then stopped. "No one has ever needed me," he confided.

He paused. In the quiet, a lump forming in my throat, I tried to think of something reassuring to say to him. But Paul spoke first.

"But you don't have to worry, Kathy," he said. "I need you. I need all of you."

When we got back to his room, we started up the Stevie again on his CD player. I didn't know how to work it, but Paul did. He didn't have a room-mate anymore, so we could blast it. We sat on the beds and listened for a bit, me on the blue striped spread and Paul on his blanket. Paul began bouncing his shoulders and snapping his fingers, so I got up and pulled him to his feet, and then we danced a sort of Lindy together.

"For as long as I know I have love I can make it..." we sang along as we danced. I twirled myself under his arm and reached to catch his hand again.

But he stopped, fell onto his bed gasping for breath, and held his hand to his chest.

22. Andromeda

It was a little after eleven o'clock on a cold, rainy March night. I was just getting into bed when my phone rang. Paul had taken a turn for the worse. I called Patrick and asked him to meet me, then dressed and hurried through the rain to Westledge.

When the elevator door opened on Paul's floor, I could make out Patrick leaning over a gurney near the nurses' station, his hand over his eyes.

The hallway was dark and quiet. The nurse on duty looked up from the lamp-lit desk. "Katherine? Over here," she said in a hoarse whisper, waving me toward her and nodding at Patrick and the gurney.

Patrick looked up. His face was drawn and wrinkled.

How had my younger brothers gotten so old?

"We're praying," Patrick said.

"He's doing better," the nurse murmured as I approached. "We're giving him a nebulizer treatment."

Paul's gurney was adjusted so he was half-sitting up, but his face was almost covered by a clear plastic mask. He was gasping in it, his eyes wide with fear.

Patrick said, "I told him the Lord is watching over him."

So some god let this illness take his sanity, looked the other way for years when caretakers gave him cigarettes to be quiet, and now is going to start looking over him? I bit my lip.

Paul moved the mask to one side. "You're here, Kathy!" he said.

"Shh. Keep your mask on," I said and I kissed him on the forehead. He lay back, but pushed the mask aside again.

170

"I don't want to die," he said, his lip trembling.

"I know," I said. I rubbed his hands to warm them, then tucked them under his blanket. Mother's hands were cold, too, that last day in the emergency room.

The nurse looked back down at her notes. An old woman's voice was calling. "I want to go home," the woman said. "Please. Call my daughter. She'll come and take me home." An aide swished by on rubber-soled shoes and hurried into a room down the hall. A door closed quietly.

"Monica was here this afternoon," Patrick said. "She brought him some pizza. Right kiddo?"

Paul nodded. "I don't want to die," he repeated. It echoed inside the mask. He sounded as though he were under water.

Patrick bent over him again and stroked his arms under the thin blanket. "Just think. Our heavenly father is waiting to welcome you into heaven," he said. "And Mother and Daddy are there waiting for you."

"And Charlie, too?" The words were muffled, as if from far away.

Patrick hesitated.

"Sure he is," I said. "He's waiting to play fetch with you."

Paul closed his eyes and grew calm.

***

It was the next day, or the day after that. A nurse technician placed a placebo bandage on the angry, red, golf-ball sized lump that had erupted from his chest.

"Can't they just cut it off?" Paul asked. He fingered it gingerly. It itched.

It was odd; since the chemo stopped his hair had begun to grow back. He didn't look that bad until you saw his chest.

"Can't it be removed?" I asked the radiologist when I caught her alone.

171

"It is larger inside than it is outside," she said. "There's nothing we can do."

***

When I get home after a day with Paul I pace from room to room, or stand at the window watching neighbors drive home from wherever they've been for the afternoon. One by one the Hondas, Toyotas and BMWs slip into garages. Lights glow from kitchen windows. At our birdfeeder, nuthatches and chickadees grab a late afternoon snack in their little tuxedos.

Outside my front window a doe and
her fawn are nibbling on what's left
of my Weigela and Andromeda bushes.

With dusk the moon slips up into the trees.
They cast long shadows on the snow, and
the stars of the Andromeda galaxy glow,

flickering from 2.2 million light years away
-- about how far God could travel in an instant
if what the nuns taught us were true.

Yet the deer eat away at my landscaping,
the cancer eats away at Paul's insides,
and God does nothing.

23. Bon Voyage

From: Ilene Wells
To: Sheila Flannery, Katherine Dering, Charlotte Flannery, Grace Flannery, Laurie Flannery, Patrick Flannery, Monica Leggett, Julia Brower, Loretta Pontillo, Charlotte Pontillo, Melissa Leggett, Shelly Flannery, Sean Flannery, Kerry Flannery, John Flannery, Russell Leggett, Meghan Mahoney, Lucy Lesperance,
Date: Wednesday, February 27, 2008 8:46 PM
Subject: Let's all get together

Hey everyone,

Let's try to figure out when would be a good time for a Flannery reunion. I have this burning need to get all ten of us together as soon as possible. With this recent news about Paul on top of my near miss car accident and last year's scare with Johnny's aneurism, I am really afraid that we will lose our chance for the ten of us to be together while we still can. Who knows what could happen and then we'll regret we didn't get together.

Let's figure out what time would work out for everyone. Charlotte suggested Easter. I was thinking Memorial Day weekend.

Love, Ilene

Re: Let's all get together
Date: Thursday, February 28, 2008 6:29 PM
From: Monica Leggett

I'd love to do a family party but my weekends are out of control in April and May. I have weddings, showers, graduation, you name it.

I may be the limiting factor for things--if you have to schedule without me I'll do my best to be there. How about June 14th? Laurie, when do you get done with school?

Marmee Monica

Re: Let's all get together
Date: Thursday, February 28, 2008 7:18 PM
From: Grace Flannery

I'm scheduled to do a workshop in Boston over Memorial Day weekend, but if that is the best choice I will try to get someone else to take my place. What about the weekend of May 3-4? Would that work for everyone?

Grace

Re: Let's all get together

Date: Thursday, February 28, 2008 8:24 PM
From: Patrick Flannery

Wow! That's quite a mailstorm! (hah hah)

After dozens of emails trying to plan a big summer party, ranging from boat rides to a James Bond party (the men would wear tuxes) to trips to Lake Welch, Ilene finally pointed out that Paul might not last till June. Johnny was considering coming up the weekend Grace planned to visit, March 14 - 17. We decided on a get-together that weekend, which eventually morphed into a St. Patrick's Day party at my house.

We prepared for the day in a state of tearful mania. Who has CD's of Irish music? Tommy Makem, Irish Rovers, Celtic Thunder, whatever. Anything to pretend this wasn't a farewell party for Paul.

***

When I was in college at Le Moyne, a little Jesuit college in upstate New York, St. Pat's was an excuse to cut class and get drunk by noon. We'd escape our pasteurized campus and head downtown to the seedy old bars near Syracuse University, where old Polish diehards led the juke box with their swizzle sticks through an alcoholic haze. The bars' sagging corners had filled with 50 years of tobacco ashes and assorted debris till all was rounded and a dingy grey.

In honor of the heaviest drinking day of the year, the owners supplemented the usual jukebox choices of Otis Redding, Aretha Franklin, Janis Joplin and the Rolling Stones with the three or four Irish groups popular with college drinkers. In our crowd, Jimmy, Murph the Surf and Eddie would lead the group, singing along with Tommy and the lads.

My girlfriends and I would sit at the grimy bar across from the enormous jar of pickled eggs and eat hot dogs steamed in beer to get a "good base" for the serious drinking that was soon to follow. For a day the gang would leave behind our neat cinderblock dormitories and matching sweater and skirt sets to wallow in sweat shirts and dirty blue jeans, singing Irish drinking songs and drinking green beer. One year Eddie and Ratzo dyed their pet guinea pig green and hitched to New York City for the big parade. They were missing for a week.

Paul went missing in 1976 and never came back.

***

Our party for Paul was a more subdued, afternoon family affair. John and Grace made it in from North Carolina and

175

California. It was mostly family, but a few friends from the old neighborhood showed up. Paul seemed to rally for the occasion. He didn't care for the corned beef, but he had a huge plate of mac and cheese and at least two ice cream sundaes.

Paul beamed all day

Johnny and Patrick played their guitars and we all joined in and sang old favorite songs. We took lots of pictures.

John and Patrick

The nieces and nephews were sweet. They made a real effort to overcome their fear of Paul. They all understood how important it was to their mothers. Thanks, kids!

Cousins, l to r: Nora, Katie, Christine and Clare (Nick hiding behind Nora)

Back, l to r: Patrick, Charlotte, Sheila, Paul, Ilene Front: John, Katherine, Julia, Grace, Monica

Paparazzi

Fwd.: Re: Paul
Date: Sunday, March 16, 2008 6:30 PM
From: Ilene

Be prepared to cry...
This is Paul's 9th Grade Highlands yearbook picture. I lost my yearbook and asked to get a copy of it from a classmate of mine...I thought you'd all like to see it. He was so handsome...

Ilene

The next few weeks were tough.

One day I picked Paul up at his nursing home for a doctor's appointment. Today was a pre-radiation checkup, which should have only taken about ten minutes, but when we got to Dr. Ayan's office, the waiting room was jammed. He was running late, as usual. We waited an hour and a half for our time with the good doctor. Paul got up three or four times to use the rest room, where mostly he just stood in front of the mirror with the door open making faces at himself and mumbling conversations with someone no one else could see. Practicing the old mojo. He came back to his seat in the waiting room with his straggly hair pushed this way or that.

After he finally saw the doctor and got the go ahead for the next round of radiation, we were hungry and thirsty. Today he opted for the Chinese restaurant down the street. He ordered his now familiar shrimp egg foo yung. I asked him if there was anything he'd like to do before going back. "Let's just ride around," he said. I steered us toward the riverfront park.

He told me one time that at Harlem Valley Hospital, where he spent about fifteen years, and at Hudson River Psychiatric, where he spent three years or so, he liked to stand at the window and try to catch sight of the trains going by or watch cars pulling in and out of the visitors' lot.

Today, we sat in the park and watched the trains for a while, then shot up to the bridge to see if there were any hawks or eagles out riding the currents before heading back to Westledge.

The next weeks were a downhill glide. A couple more scans, radiation on the growth that was bothering him, and lots of visits to the diners, but Paul faded out, like an eastern afternoon sky, a little less light every minute.

24. Visiting

From: Ilene Wells

To: "Charlotte Flannery, Charlotte Pontillo, Christine Leggett, Grace Flannery, Greg Wells, Johnny Flannery, Julia Flannery Brower, Katherine Dering, Kerry Flannery, Laurie Flannery, Loretta Pontillo, Melissa Leggett, Monica Leggett, Patrick Flannery, Roy Wells, Russell Leggett, Sean Flannery, Sheila Flannery, Shelley Flannery, Emily Ra'ed" ...more

Date: March 23, 2008 10:07 PM

Subject: A good day

It was a good day. John and Tim (Paul's best friends from childhood - for those of you that haven't been in the loop) met me at West Ledge at 1:30 and waited in the lobby while I went up to get Paul. They were very sorry to hear that Paul was so sick and thankful that they could see him again.

I told Paul that I had a surprise for him waiting in the lobby - in fact two surprises. I was holding my breath a little because I wasn't sure how Paul would react when he saw them. I thought he might be very self-conscious. He didn't recognize John at first. He called him Scott, but when John said who he was, Paul immediately gave him a big hug and called him "Carno!" - he looked so happy to see him. He then gave Tim just as big of a hug and they immediately started sharing stories. John brought out his framed picture of the Bernies, the football team he played on with Paul and many neighborhood friends. He promised to get a copy made for Paul.

We went to the New City Diner and the stories kept flowing. Paul kept up with them very well - he was even able to fill in some of the blanks and John and Tim were amazed at his memory. He <u>did</u> add the usual Paul touches, of events that never happened, but they were so good with Paul; they didn't once seem like they felt awkward and I could tell that it helped Paul feel comfortable around them - comfortable enough to talk about getting shot in the back of his head by Dickie and about other things that didn't happen - and they didn't even blink an eye.

We were there for two hours and the time flew by. Eventually, I noticed Paul was rubbing the side of his head and I asked him how he was doing. He said he was a little tired and so we headed back to West Ledge. We chatted a little more in the parking lot and I took this picture. John got Paul to smile with something funny he said. They both said that they would like to try and visit Paul some more. I told them that it would be great for him to have some male companionship and for him to just let me know when. They both thought Paul was much better than the last time they saw him. I guess they went up to Wingdale one time and Paul was pretty out of it. They actually thought Paul looked pretty good.

John, Paul and Tim

You should have seen Paul's face. He really lit up the whole time they were together, as you can see by this picture. He was very happy when he went back to his room. I'm sure he'll be talking about this for a long time.
 I also feel confident that John and Tim will follow through with more visits.
So, it was a very good day.

Ilene

I got a phone call to come see the social worker, Sharon. It was time to get some paperwork done, she told me. It would make things easier when the time came. We needed to pick out a funeral home and we needed Paul to sign forms. We needed a do-not-resuscitate order, and she wanted him to name a couple of us to his health care proxy. I was afraid talking about it would freak him out. I hoped he wouldn't go off on us and rant in Sharon's office.

I felt a bit disjointed. I had done little beyond caring for Paul for months. But during the winter I had started taking a Tai Chi class. We met Tuesday and Thursday mornings from 10 to 11, and I blanked out for an hour, focusing on the moves, breathing slowly, new-agey, vaguely oriental music in the background, with flutes and an oriental string instrument, the occasional little bell chime. My arms moving in a slow wave, knee up, turn, hold and balance.

Usually then I changed my clothes, drove to Peekskill and picked up Paul for lunch. Radiation treatments ended a few weeks ago, and we were in a kind of limbo. Paul's doctors wanted more tests done before they decided on the next course of treatment. I needed a rest. I needed to get away from this. But how much worse was it for Paul?

Sharon met Monica and me in her office just off the reception area on the first floor. She got right into what needed

182

to be done, pulling out a folder already set with the needed forms and rummaging through her file cabinet for others.

Paul's file sat on her desk. It looked so pitiful. Could we really be preparing for his death? He was only 48.

Sharon saw the look on my face. "Don't feel bad," she said. "At least Paul isn't an NKR."

I gave her a puzzled look.

"You know, NKRs? They're the ones with no known relatives," she explained. She slammed some papers on her desk. "What? Do they grow on trees, these poor people? They're people like your brother, but their families have abandoned them. We try to make them as comfortable as we can, but there's no way we can make up for how alone they feel in this world." Her eyes glistened with the tears she would not shed.

"You girls have been wonderful to him," she said.

Now I teared up. I felt like such a fraud. All I could remember now were the years that I hardly ever visited him, the times we didn't let him come to holidays because the teenage girls were afraid of him. But over this past year, he surprised me almost every visit. The reincarnation discussion, the blissful enjoyment of a simple day in the sun – I felt embarrassed I hadn't taken better care of him before. If Monica and Ilene hadn't pushed, would I have encouraged him this much?

Monica nodded silently and bit her lip. I said, "Thank you. We do our best."

Just then Paul popped in. "Hey, I didn't know you guys were here," he said, kissing Monica and me. "Are we going out?" His hair was combed and his clothes, clean. "I'll go get my coat," he said.

"Whoa, we have to do some paperwork first," Sharon said. She asked him to sit.

He was smiling, calm.

"Your sisters are pretty good to you, aren't they?" she

began.

"Yeah. They are so good. It's unbelievable how good they have been," he said, his head nodding up and down. "They're my mothers."

He turned to me. "You *are* my mother, Kathy. I mean, you know that, right?" He smiled benignly, hands in his lap, not a care in the world.

Sharon nodded. "If you were unconscious, Paul. Or something. Or if there was something complicated going on, you'd trust them to talk with the doctors or tell the doctors what to do, wouldn't you?"

Paul furrowed his brows, thinking. "Well, of course," he said.

"Well, we need you to sign this piece of paper that says that. Would you be willing to sign that?" she asked.

"Sure I would," he said.

She handed him a pen.

He signed. "That's it? Is that why you asked me to come down?

"That's it. That's all I needed. And now you can go out," she said. We all laughed.

"What kind of ice cream do you want?" Monica asked.

From: Katherine Dering
To: Monica Leggett, Patrick Flannery, sheila flannery , Julia flannery Brower, Grace Flannery, Johnny Flannery, Laurie flannery, Kerry flannery, Charlotte Flannery, Sean Flannery , shelley Flannery, Melissa Leggett, Christine Leggett, russell Leggett, Charlotte Pontillo, Loretta Pontillo , Meghan Mahoney Von Hofe, Ilene Wells, Lucy Lesperance... more
Date: Thursday, April 10, 2008 7:07
Subject: Re: Paul bad news

Grace is visiting. She and I took Paul to see Dr. Khosa today. Dr. Ayan is on vacation. Paul had fallen twice this AM before we got there and was in a wheelchair. But he actually looked pretty good and was in a good mood and was able to walk to the car. We gave Dr. K. an update on the PET scan and the brain scan and she reviewed the notes from Westledge on Paul's condition, including blood counts.

Dr. Khosa undid the bandage over the lump on his chest and found that it is now oozing. She recommended that they radiate it. She said surgery would require painful skin grafts, and the radiation alone should shrink it back to almost nothing in three weeks or so. So that will begin on Monday. I've ordered ambulette service. Monica and I can meet him there and drive him home and out for ice cream or whatever.

While Paul was getting his measurements done so they could set up the radiation equipment, Grace and I spoke with Dr. Khosa I said, "He's not going to make it, is he?"
And she said, "No, he isn't."

Grace and I checked out a funeral home in Katonah afterwards. (at Sharon's suggestion). It was pretty expensive, and neither of us thought it was really that nice, although the director seemed nice to work with, and it was in a convenient location. I will check out a couple more. Ilene, Grace and I think that having a short service at the funeral home, with the priest that Paul knows from the nursing home leading the service, would probably be good. No need for the falderol of a funeral mass like we had for Mother. It doesn't sound like he will make it through the summer, so we should plan ahead. When the time is right, Monica or I may find the right way to ask Paul what he wants. We'll see.

In the meantime, the health care proxy and DNR are in place.

  Ciao
  K

From: Charlotte Flannery

To: Monica Leggett, Patrick Flannery, sheila flannery , Katherine Dering, Julia flannery Brower, Grace Flannery, Johnny Flannery, Laurie flannery, Kerry flannery, Charlotte Flannery, Sean Flannery , Shelley Flannery, Melissa Leggett, Christine Leggett, russell Leggett, Charlotte Pontillo, Loretta Pontillo , Meghan Mahoney, Ilene Wells, Roy Wells, Russell Leggett, Lucy Lesperance... more

Date: Thursday, April 17, 2008 2:39 PM

Subject: Re: Paul

Paul is declining rapidly. He is on oxygen all the time now. He has a portable oxygen tank for when he goes to the doctor, but still he is weaker than ever and will soon need a wheelchair. He still enjoys eating and drinking! He doesn't have much energy for it though. Today when we went to the park for a picnic he didn't want to get out of the car. He complained of being cold (even though it was hot) and closed his eyes a lot. I drove to a spot where you could see the water and he didn't even seem interested in opening his eyes to look at it. He found it difficult walking from the car to the nursing home elevator and was breathing hard, seemed anxious to lie down. Back in his room he lay down without even taking his coat off. He seemed a bit better after resting in his bed for a while but still, too little energy to talk much.

We need to think about the next phase.

Should we stop the radiation treatments soon (now)? The only point was to dry up/shrink that tumor on his chest a bit because it bothered him. I don't think it bothers him as much now. Also, the trips are getting hard on him.

We will be calling in the hospice service soon. Do we need to ALL consult on and agree to the details? The plan we are considering would mean no more trips to the hospital, no IV hydration, etc.

I know that Paul really enjoys seeing everyone even though at this point the visits will be short and uneventful. As I mentioned, he still enjoys eating and drinking. He had a yogurt and a half a sandwich with me today and some Entemans Apple Puffs, too (cut up into small pieces). He enjoys the vitamin water drinks and also asked for orange juice.

        Love to all,
        Charlotte

From: Charlotte Flannery
To: Monica Leggett, Patrick Flannery, sheila flannery , Katherine Dering, Julia flannery Brower, Grace Flannery, Johnny Flannery, Laurie flannery, Kerry flannery, Charlotte Flannery, Sean Flannery , shelley Flannery, Melissa Leggett, Christine Leggett, russell Leggett, Charlotte Pontillo, Loretta Pontillo , Meghan Mahoney Von Hofe, Ilene Wells, Roy Wells, Russell Leggett, Lucy Lesperance... more
Date: Friday, April 18, 2008 5:45 PM
Subject: Paul had a good day

Paul was much better today. We went to the diner for brunch after the doctor's. We talked about what to do after eating and he still didn't think he was up to any walking, not even from the car to a bench. He did want to go for a ride and we decided to go to White Plains. The first place he wanted to go was to his old apartment in WP and he walked right into the old Search for Change office and asked if he could get his old apartment back. He also asked if anyone knew what happened to Marty. The rest of the time he stayed in the car. When we got back to the nursing home he was tired but not exhausted the way he was on Wednesday. Let's hope he has more good days like today.

From: Patrick Flannery

To: Monica Leggett, Patrick Flannery, sheila flannery , Katherine Dering, Julia flannery Brower, Grace Flannery, Johnny Flannery, Laurie flannery, Kerry flannery, Charlotte Flannery, Sean Flannery , shelley Flannery, Melissa Leggett, Christine Leggett, russell Leggett, Charlotte Pontillo, Loretta Pontillo , Meghan Mahoney, Ilene Wells, Roy Wells, Russell Leggett, Lucy Lesperance, Suzanne Gillespie... more

Date: Friday, April 18, 2008 9:15 PM

Subject: Paul had a good day

Hi, all,

I dropped by after work and visited for about an hour. I brought him a milk shake, which he consumed with gusto. He seemed more energetic than I'd expected, but Charlotte's email kind of explains that: He has felt uprooted, but now he was back in the old stomping grounds, which always feels good, I think. He asked about Timmy and Carno. He didn't get up from his bed, however, and he started to doze toward the end, so I made my good nights.

I added cousin Suzanne to the grand list, let's keep her in the loop.

Pat

From: Katherine Dering

To: Monica Leggett, Patrick Flannery, sheila flannery , Julia flannery Brower, Grace Flannery, Johnny Flannery, Laurie flannery, Kerry flannery, Charlotte Flannery, Sean Flannery , shelley Flannery, Melissa Leggett, Christine Leggett, russell Leggett, Charlotte Pontillo, Loretta Pontillo , Meghan Mahoney, Ilene Wells, Roy Wells, Russell Leggett, Lucy Lesperance, Suzanne Gillespie... more

Date: Monday, April 21, 2008 10:17 AM

Subject: Paul back from the ER

188

I got a call at about 11:30 last night that they were sending Paul to the ER, for confusion and tremors, jerky motions. Sheila was visiting overnight; we were still up gabbing, so we both went to check up on things. They called back before we left to say they were taking him to Phelps Memorial Hospital, in Sleepy Hollow, because Hudson Valley Hospital Center was full.

At Phelps, Paul had arrived dressed - he had his boots on. But he was kind of mumbling and babbling. They ran tests on him - Xray, brain scan, blood work. Ox of 80-83 while I was watching. (should be 97-98) slightly elevated white blood count, x-ray showed an interior tumor bigger than the one that shows - the size of a baseball, he said, and no tumors in the brain.

I was glad we were there, because they haven't treated Paul before, and they didn't know whether this is how he usually is, or if he's better or worse. No one sent his records, so they were running every test you could think of.

I had nice chats with Johnny (by phone) and both doctors there. Bottom line: there was nothing they could do for him at the hospital that they can't do at Westledge. I asked Paul when he first got there what I could do for him and he said, "I don't want to die." He was scared. But then he babbled for a while. I really don't know what he was mumbling. Later, I asked again, and he wanted water, some more mumbly, and to go back to Westledge. Sheila got him an extra blanket and he leaned back and dozed off.

We discussed hospice with the docs, and they said Westledge's comfort care service would be the right thing to do. If we don't, every time Paul mumbles, or falls, or his o2 count falls to 80, they're going to send him to the emergency room and wake me or Monica up. And it just scares him and doesn't help. So we'll be talking with Renata about getting him moved to that unit today.

No more radiation.

Sheila and I got home from the hospital at about 3 am and I couldn't sleep. My head was spinning. Paul had, indeed, had a lousy turn this time around.

Some days, I could hardly remember before this all started. I had finally quit my job. I seldom saw my friends. I hardly ever even saw my sisters, unless we took a turn with Paul together, like Sheila and I did tonight. About the only outside human contact I had was with a writing class at the Hudson Valley Writers' Center. I'd been working on a memoir about being a pioneer senior female officer in corporate America. The class was supposed to help me organize it and finish it. But I couldn't seem to focus on it. The writers' center looks out over the Hudson River, and I kept seeing all my little excursions with Paul. All I seemed to be able to write were little sketches about our visits – hawks, Stevie, coughing cancer away, the good life.

Re: Paul back from the ER
From: Monica
Date: Monday, April 21, 2008 11:14 AM

It's 11am and I just called Dr. Khosa's office to see if anyone had told them about Paul. They didn't know why he hadn't come for his radiation. I let them know about the size of the internal tumor and that he wouldn't be coming for any more radiation.
  Lori (the secretary), said to tell everyone that they offer prayers and best wishes to all of us, and to Paul of course. I told her that we really appreciated everything that they had done for Paul and how great they had treated him. I'm going to call Dr. Khosa at her other office to let her know.
  Katherine, call me when you're awake.

Monica

From: Pat C.
To: Katherine, Rachel, Janet, Carole, Diana, Maggie, more...
Date: Wednesday, April 23, 2008 10:02 PM
Subject: Paul

Hi Everyone,
 I got word from Katherine. Her brother, Paul, has taken a turn for the worse. Please keep her family in your prayers. I will call her during the day and send word to you.
 Pat

Date: Thursday, April 24, 2008 10:58 AM
From: Carole

Hi Katherine,

 Pat has kept me posted about Paul; I am so sorry. Please know that you and your family are in my thoughts -- and that I'm always here if you would like to talk.
 Take care -- and much love,
Carole

A couple of days after the late night emergency room visit, Sheila and I drove to Westledge to take Paul to the oncologist. He was scheduled to get his second round of treatment with "Alempt," today, the second choice chemotherapy that the doctor thought Paul should try when the primary chemo treatment failed.

It was sunny out, but cold and windy. Inside the nursing home, old ladies sitting in their wheel chairs met us as the elevator doors opened. Sheila went to the desk to sign him out, and I headed down to Paul's room. Paul was already wearing

191

his black leather jacket, his favorite belonging after the DVD player. He was sitting quietly by the window in a wheel chair, but he brightened when he saw me. "I had another spill," he explained about the wheelchair, smiling. "My legs don't seem to work right."

"Well, we'll just have to help you out, then. I'll push you, and then you can hold on to me when we get to Dr. Ayan's office, okay?"

We wheeled him to the front door, and he walked to Sheila's car. Sheila drove up close to the doctor's office, and I helped him out. He walked slowly, but seemed to get his legs back as he went. He walked unassisted to the restroom twice during the twenty minutes in the waiting room and came back with his hair wet and sticking up this way and that. Still checking to make sure nothing was missing.

The three of us met with the doctor and gave him the rundown on our midnight ride to Phelps Memorial two days before. After examining Paul and reading through the results of tests run at the emergency room, the doctor motioned to me to come and speak with him in another room. Leaving Paul with Sheila, I sat with the doctor, listening to him hem and haw about scarce resources and obligations and concentrating treatments on patients who might benefit most from them.

From the beginning, this doctor had seemed a little uneasy about devoting time and attention to Paul. Coming from the third world, where medicines are in such short supply, he seemed to wonder about taking such care with someone as disabled as Paul. You could usually see it in his eyes – detached, head to one side, not trying to accommodate the need to approach Paul gently.

But today, his reluctance was based on the poor prognosis, not the relative value of Paul's life, and it seemed justified. I cut him off, sparing him the agony of trying to say that he didn't think we should be giving Paul any more

192

treatments. "He's not going to get better, is he?" I asked.

He shook his head and launched into another, mostly unintelligible round of "squamus cell" and "rate of growth" and "carcinomas." I again cut him off. If Monica had been there, she would have taken notes. I had a ringing in my ears.

"How long does he have?" I asked.

He shook his head again. "Not long," he said. I finally pinned him down to a couple of weeks, max. "He should really be in hospice now," he said.

I nodded and start to rise, to go back to Paul and Sheila.

"Wait. I want to tell you what to expect," he said. "You have to know."

I sat back into my chair and he detailed how the end would likely happen, with Paul gasping for air like a beached fish, or delirious with pneumonia, or choking on food because the tumor was blocking off his trachea.

"His weakness in his hands, his wobbly walk – He's not getting oxygen to his muscles," he said. "It will just get worse."

I'd been the strong one till now. Practical, organized. Spreadsheets and timetables. Visiting three funeral homes in one afternoon – the smell of lilies and whatever that perfume is that they use in funeral homes was in my nose for days. I remembered sitting at my father's bedside at the end, feeding him applesauce. He smacked his lips like the babies used to do. It took Dad six weeks of gasping to finally succumb to the last stages of emphysema. I pictured Paul gasping like that. I couldn't hold it in any longer. I burst into tears.

It took a while for me to compose myself before going back into the room where Paul and Sheila were waiting. The doctor sat with me. We didn't usually meet in this office. I didn't know whose it was. It was pretty much like Dr. Ayan's. The same shoddy desk and chairs. I thought of all the people who had sat in these chairs hoping for good news, most of them getting bad news. I wondered how I would tell Paul what the doctor had just said. I panicked that I wouldn't remember and wished I had written some of it down.

But when the doctor and I went back, the doctor seemed to look at Paul differently. I read sympathy in his face. Paul was practically skin and bones despite all our attempts to stuff him with burgers and milk shakes. I think it may be the first time that the doctor really saw Paul as a person, not a schizophrenic, or a nameless stage 3B lung cancer case.

"I've brought Katherine up to date on everything," he said to Sheila and Paul. "We won't be doing any more chemo right now. I'll leave instructions for care with Paul's doctor at Westledge."

Sheila sent me worried eyebrows and grimaces when she thought Paul wasn't looking. When we left the office, Paul tottered over to the doctor and thanked him for all his efforts. The doctor smiled at Paul and they shook hands, the doctor holding Paul's arm in his left hand as he shook the hand with his right.

"I'm sorry," the doctor said. And then he turned away.

Paul managed to walk all the way to the car and seemed interested in Sheila's suggestion of a picnic at the riverfront park, where we'd gone so many times over the past year. With foot long sandwiches, sodas and chips from Subway, the three of us sat on a wrought iron bench looking out over the river. A train whistled as it pulled into the Peekskill station.

Paul finally asked, "So what did he say?"

I explained that the chemo wasn't working, that the radiation wasn't working, that he had two more tumors, and that the doctor said there was nothing more he could do. There would be no more doctor visits.

Paul pursed his lips and stared across the river. There were no boats out today. "Well then," he said. "I guess I'll have to cure myself."

A hawk soared slowly overhead, making great wide

circles, looking for dinner, I presume.

Paul ate little of his sandwich and chips.

Sheila and I made short work of ours, then fed the leftovers to the gulls that had appeared the minute our paper bag of food was brandished.

Paul was very quiet on the ride back to Westledge, his usual optimism gone. He lay down in his bed and closed his eyes as soon as we got back and didn't want to talk.

It's an odd thing, this dying. We Northerners, especially, should have learned by now that our time will be gone in the blink of an eye.

My cat Brownie was fifteen when her mottled, tortoise-shelled coat lost its lovely sheen. I think about her on this cold spring day, as I consider our human cross-over rituals: the denial, the painful procedures, the no-win decisions.

Brownie lay for days stretched out by the wood stove, gasping for breath, sides heaving. But she purred in my lap as we drove to the vet's, where soothing voices, gentle strokes and a tiny prick eased her off to her journey through the Milky Way.

But we humans lose grandparents, then parents, and still, like snakes, we shed our skins each spring and slither off to the next sunny rock to bake, to cure. We're oblivious, deluded, astonished when sharp talons come from nowhere, and just like that we're off to meet eternity.

I made my email report to everyone with the bad prognosis as soon as I got back home. Patrick decided to visit

Paul after work to keep him company with the news. When he arrived, Paul was lying very still in his bed, still dressed, his boots still on, Navajo blanket to his chin, his dinner tray untouched. The first words he said to Pat were, "I don't want to die."

"I know," Patrick said, running his hand over Paul's shoulder. "But don't worry, Mother and Daddy will be waiting in heaven for you."

"And Grandma and Charlie too?" Paul asked.

Leaving his conservative Christian beliefs to one side, Patrick reconfirmed that yes, Charlie would be waiting there for him, too.

Paul dozed off while Pat sat there, and he stayed for an hour or so

When he woke up, Pat found him a soda and some ice cream from the nurses' station and later helped him to undress and get to the bathroom. He stayed till Paul fell asleep.

25. Reunion

From: Katherine Dering

To: Monica Leggett, Patrick Flannery, sheila flannery , Julia flannery Brower, Grace Flannery, Johnny Flannery, Laurie flannery, Kerry flannery, Charlotte Flannery, Sean Flannery , shelley Flannery, Melissa Leggett, Christine Leggett, Roy Wells, russell Leggett, Charlotte Pontillo, Loretta Pontillo , Meghan Mahoney, Ilene Wells, Lucy Lesperance, Suzanne Gillespie, Barbara Reitman,... more

Date Saturday, April 26, 2008 9:19 PM

Subject Marty and Paul

Sheila, Monica and I visited with Paul on Thursday. Sheila had located Paul's old roommate, Marty, and she brought him up from White Plains to visit. They were roommates for 18 years! We ate at the New City Diner and then went to the river front park. Paul got pretty tired, but was obviously happy to see Marty. We fed the geese a little and watched the river in front of us and the trains behind us. I printed out pix at the CVS, and Marty clutched his like they were gold. Sheila and Monica took Paul back. I drove Marty back to White Plains, and the whole way back, he kept saying "Seeing Paul was a dream come true. I'm going to put these pictures in my strong box the minute I get home." Monica took a couple to put in Paul's album.

I spoke with Westledge - with Renata, the chief administrator - and told her that Dr. Ayan had prescribed Hospice care from here on out. She will get that started.

We saw Dr. Ayan on Wednesday, and he says that there's a really large tumor that has caused the right upper lobe to collapse. (that's the baseball size one) Also, there's a 2.5 centimeter mass in the left lower lung. So that's three that are big enough to see. And the lymph nodes are enlarged. Ayan says they are probably pressing on the trachea, depending on how Paul is sitting or lying.

He estimates that within the next three or four weeks, Paul's decline will be dramatic and rapid. Friday Julia visited Paul and called me while they were out - they were on their way to get ice cream sodas.

Don't forget, everyone, to pick up the portable oxygen tank and bring it with you when you take Paul out. If we had it with us when we were out with Marty, Paul would have enjoyed the day more.

Ilene and Charlotte are taking him out today. That's all for now.

Katherine

From: Charlotte Flannery
Date: Saturday, April 26, 2008 11:08 PM

Subject: Re Paul

Katherine and Pat are with Paul now. It sounds like he is mostly the same as how he was this afternoon...weak, mumbling... The night nurse hadn't seen Paul for a few weeks and so was unprepared for the extent of his decline. Katherine and Pat will take turns staying with Paul tonight. Ilene will go to the nursing home first thing in the morning.
        –Charlotte

From: Katherine Dering
    To: Monica Leggett, Patrick Flannery, sheila flannery , Julia flannery Brower, Grace Flannery, Johnny Flannery, Laurie flannery, Kerry flannery, Charlotte Flannery, Sean Flannery , shelley Flannery, Melissa Leggett, Christine Leggett, Roy Wells, russell Leggett, Charlotte Flannery, Charlotte Pontillo, Loretta Pontillo , Meghan Mahoney, Ilene Wells, Lucy Lesperance, Suzanne Gillespie, Barbara Reitman, jennifer dering... more
    Date Sunday, April 27, 2008 10:09 AM
    Subject: Paul

Patrick and I stayed with Paul till about midnight last night. He was very groggy at first, and seemed to sleep deeply for the first hour or so. His blood O2 was only 81-83, so he was pretty foggy. A couple of nurses from other floors came by to visit with him and told us how much they like him, that he's such a nice guy. I don't think Paul knew they were there. But Patrick noticed he tried to open his eyes when we talked about Carno. So he's not really asleep, I don't think.

Then he tried to get up three or four times and almost landed on his head. Even with us right there, it was hard to keep him from falling. He wakes with a start and tries to bolt out of bed. He is quite disoriented and sort of

199

flops around. At one point he noticed it was me standing there, and he said, "Katherine! Are you going to take me out?" as if it was time to go for ice cream. I said, not right now. But mostly he didn't make any sense. Patrick helped him into the bathroom a couple of times, and he sat up to cough up phlegm a couple of times.

The days are blurring together. Didn't I already send this email a couple of times?

We let the nurses know how he was, and that Pat and I would be going home soon. They didn't have enough staff to have someone sit with him in his room full time. They said Paul is often up and down during the night and likes to hang around and chat with them, so they put him into a wheelchair and propped him up near them, with his oxygen machine. (That's where he was when Pat and I got there, also). I think they do this routinely with someone they're afraid will fall. He had a couple of glasses of juice and looked comfortable enough when we left. He mumbled that he loved us when we said good bye.

I suspect this confusion and babbling and sudden flopping around is going to go on until the end, which I think we can all hope will come soon.

      Katherine

The next time I saw him, Paul had a Band-Aid on his forehead and a huge bruise on his forearm. "I had a little spill," he said.

"He's having a lot of spills," the nurse-in-charge said.

Charlotte called in sick to work and spent the better part of two days sitting with him and holding him down.

We hired aides to sit with him 24/7.

26. Indians

Original drawing by David Laing Dawson

It was almost May. There were no more treatments, no more trips to the emergency room. We were just keeping him comfortable now. I'd spent all day at the office, called in to help my replacement handle a big project. Afterwards, I came by Westledge and found Paul sitting with his aide, Jonathan, in the activity room. A tiny little old lady sat motionless in another chair. The TV was tuned to a game show; lights blinked and a buzzer sounded.

"Kathy!" Paul said, and tried to rise from his wheel chair. He almost fell. "Are we going to go out?"

"Whoa," Jonathan said, catching him. "I don't think you're going out this evening. Let's get you set up to visit with your sister." He wheeled Paul down the quiet hall and helped him into bed.

"My man!" Paul said, coughing, and they high fived. He lay back, exhausted. Jonathan straightened his blanket. I gave him a tissue for the spit.

"The priest came and put oil on my forehead today," Paul said. "I'm dying, aren't I?"

I didn't want to answer. He stared at me. I nodded. "We talked about this before, Paul. I wish we could change it,"

"But we can't," he finished for me. He closed his eyes.

We sat quietly.

Dings of call buttons sounded the nursing home chorus. The old man across the hall moaned.

"Hey, want some ice cream?" I taunted him, waving a small cooler I'd kept hidden.

His eyes lit up. "What kind?"

Jonathan got us a dish and spoon. But the spoon kept slipping out of his hand.

"Let me," I said, picking up the spoon and the dish. When he opened his mouth I saw the pink, toothless gums.

I remembered feeding Paul and Ilene when they were babies. I'd feed first one, then the other. My little birds. How silly the small plastic ice cream spoon looked in Paul's big mouth.

The ice cream slid off the spoon and Paul smacked his lips. Vanilla chocolate swirl. "My favorite," he said.

When we finished, he started flopping around like a fish in a boat, trying to reach something in his bedside table.

"Whoa, let me," I said. "Do you want your picture album?"

"No, my book," he said. I reached into the cabinet and found his dog-eared, junior edition of Last of the Mohicans. "Is this what you want?"

He nodded.

I put the book in his lap, and his hands stroked it

lovingly. He tried to open it, but the pages slipped from his fingers and the book dropped. Everything was slipping away from him.

"Let me help you," I said. "What are you looking for?"

"Can you find Marty and me?" he asked.

I sat on the bed next to him and held the book open, turning the pages slowly, like reading to a toddler. There were pen and ink illustrations every two or three pages. On one page was a drawing of two Native Americans in war paint. I could see Paul's gaze drawn to it.

"Is that you and Marty?" I asked.

"Yeah," he said and ran his pointer finger over Marty's face. "You know," he said, "Four score and thirty years ago, I was king of the planet." He chuckled.

All around the facing page were squiggly lines, symbols, and backward letters written in pencil and ball-point pen. He ran his finger over these, as well. I inserted a scrap of paper to help hold the book open.

We sat like that for five minutes or so, his finger barely moving over the page. He made a few soft whistles and chirps from time to time, and then he closed his eyes and lay back against the pillows. After he rested a bit, he asked for his Stevie Wonder and I set up his DVD player. When it was time to go, I kissed him on the forehead. The cut he got from his last fall wasn't healing well. I made a mental note to ask the doctor about it.

As I put my coat on, Paul was nodding to the music and gazing down at himself and Marty, back when they were kings of the forest, if not the planet. His eyes closed. I stood by the bed and watched him.

"Don't worry. We'll call you if he needs you," Jonathan said, settling into the easy chair.

Outside just then, the wind howled like marauding ghosts. A large tree by Paul's window groaned.

Outside the window a breeze swirls.
My brother stirs in his sleep
A dream hangs from his lips.

He is sane in this one.
His lungs burst with hope.
Shoulders broad and strong,

A breeze rustles the trees,
Mohicans stroll along the Hudson.
A nurse paddles her way down the hall.

I fish a tissue from the bedside,
Wipe the spittle from his dreaming lips,
Pluck a crumb from the sheets.

I fiddle in my hard little chair,
Stroke my brother's hand.
Paul's lungs succumb.

A tree branch rustles outside the window.

I slipped through the shadowy hallway and out into the rainy spring evening.

27. A Call

It was the next morning. I came home from my Tai Chi class to write out some checks for the aides before going over to the nursing home. I had set up a huge Excel spread sheet, projecting rotating shifts of aides until sometime in June, three shifts per day, name, so much per hour, times so many hours worked.

And then I got the call.

It took me a while to get to Westledge. No hurry now. I sent out an email to everyone then finished preparing last checks for the aides.

When Paul died, a paid aide was by his side. He hardly knew her. He was in yet another institutional room. All those years – thirty years of institutions – hospitals mostly, some half-way houses, a few years in that apartment with his buddy Marty, all the aides and orderlies and nurses and social workers and psychologists he'd known. And at the end it was just Pauline on her little blue chair, Valsa called in for support, and him on an air mattress supplied two days before by hospice. The oxygen concentrator rumbling. The air mattress hissing. Nurses chit-chatting in the hall.

By the time I got to Paul's room, Patrick was there. Pat and I hugged. Valsa followed me in and we hugged.

I approached Paul and stroked his cheek.

"He wasn't alone," Valsa said. "Don't worry. We were with him." A call button dinged. "I'll be just down the hall," she said.

Paul's skin was turning a waxy yellow color.

I heard a hissing sound. The oxygen concentrator, I thought, remembering Dad's. I unplugged the contraption on the floor by Paul's bed. *He doesn't need that anymore.* Pat and I rummaged through the cupboards a bit. "We'll have to sort through this," I said. "There isn't much."

"I'll take care of it," Pat said.

I turned, and Paul was sinking into the deflating mattress. He was being buried in bed linens. I hurried to plug the air mattress back in and sat and cried for a while. Patrick paced around. Slowly, Paul's body rose again.

Patrick said a couple of prayers and stroked Paul's face. An aide helped us bundle up his belongings in big plastic bags.

"Let's get out of here," I said.

Flannery, Paul, age 48 of Peekskill, NY, formerly of White Plains and graduate of White Plains High School, died peacefully at Westledge Nursing Home on May 1, 2008 after a long battle with lung cancer. He was born Christmas Day, 1959, in Geneva, Switzerland, son of the late John Edward and Mary Kay Lesperance

Flannery, long time White Plains residents. Paul was a big fan of Clint Eastwood and James Bond movies, was an avid bowler, and enjoyed his trips to the diner with family and friends.

Paul is survived by nine brothers and sisters and their spouses, Sheila Flannery and Saher Macarius of Dorchester, MA, Katherine Flannery Dering and Ken Dering of Bedford, NY, John and Laurie Flannery of Ellerbe, NC, Grace Flannery of Novato, CA, Patrick and Shelley Flannery of Katonah, NY, Charlotte Flannery of Staatsburg, NY, Monica and Steve Leggett of Shelton, CT, Paul's twin sister Ilene and her husband Willie Wells of Saugherties, NY, and Julia Flannery of Highland, NY; and 16 nieces and nephews and three great-nephews.

The family would like to thank the staff of Westledge who cared for Paul so well this past year, as well as those at Hudson Valley Hospital Center, Mahopac Radiology, Westchester Oncology, and Hedgewood Adult Home.

In lieu of flowers the family is asking that donations be sent in Paul's memory to the National Alliance for Mental Illness, P.O. Box 759155, Baltimore, MD 21275-9155.

Funeral arrangements: Viewing will be from 2-4pm and 7-9pm at Oekler & Cox Funeral Home, 262 E. Main St., Mt. Kisco, NY. Burial will take place Monday morning at Gate of Heaven Cemetery, Hawthorne, NY

28. Eulogy for Uncas

"Oh, Paul," Ilene sobbed, throwing herself onto his body. It had just arrived from the nursing home and was lying on a table in a side room at the funeral home. We let her cry for a minute or so, tears trickling down our cheeks, as well as hers, then led her into the director's office.

And there we were. Ilene, Monica, Patrick and I, sitting in the business office of "Oelker & Cox, A Sinatra Funeral Home" discussing what we wanted in the way of a funeral service for Paul. When the social worker at the nursing home suggested it might be time for us to think about such things, I had visited four different funeral homes and chose this one to set up the basic arrangements. Now it was for real, and we were sitting at this scarred old mahogany dining table in a little room off to the side of the main viewing chapel, discussing the times for the viewings and the logistics of getting Paul's body to the cemetery. We'd hit a major stumbling block: the religious part of the service.

We had never discussed any of this with Paul, as he didn't seem to want to talk about the inevitable, and I, for one, did not want to put him in a funk. He seemed content to pretend it wasn't happening.

The eighth of the ten of us, and he was the first to go.

Before the twins were born, our Swiss au pair, Elizabeth, knit a layette for the new baby on the way. She went into a panic when, six weeks before the due date, Mother went into labor early, while Dad was in South Africa. Doctors stopped the labor but found out she was carrying twins.

"Zere will be two!" Elizabeth said. She sat Sheila, Mary Grace and me down on the living room couch and told us we would have to help her knit another layette. Although the three of us were singularly unadept at any knitting, having never even tried it before, she taught us all to knit in two days. I was to make booties, Sheila the cap, Mary Grace the mittens. Elizabeth made the second sweater and pants.

That light blue yarn, the color of Paul's eyes. *Hold the yarn taut with the left hand, alongside the left needle. Flick ze right needle in and around. Move ze loop of yarn from ze left needle to ze right.* Over and over, little blue loops, through the back for a knit, through the front for a purl.

Dad rushed home. Mother lay in her bed, trying desperately not to go into labor. Elizabeth stood guard dog. *"Ze muzzer is in ze bed. You vill knit now."*

Forty-eight years later, Dad's gone, Mother's gone, Paul's gone. Now we were arranging for his funeral. Patrick brought clothes he picked out of the plastic bags of Paul's things from the nursing home. We considered burying him in a suit, but he didn't have one. He had probably never worn a suit in his life. We settled on the denim jacket that Sheila gave him, with denim pants. Patrick added one of his own white shirts. Light blue would have matched his eyes. But they wouldn't be open. We added underwear and socks.

Grace and Monica would arrange for the flowers. I would order luncheon food from a caterer.

We picked out some sappy remembrance cards. A wide variety to choose from: saints and Holy Family's, Mary in various incarnations, Jesus--all with golden haloes. "Is there anything else?" We opted for an assortment of nature pictures, in honor of Paul's one-time wish to work in the youth conservation corps. On the back of each was a poem about a butterfly coming out of its cocoon, an analogy, we hoped, for Paul being released from his prison.

Back in grade school, my girlfriends and I used to collect remembrance cards left on church pews by mourners. I especially loved the Madonna with her eyes gazing off into the heavens. I kept a file of them in my antique secretary desk of parents, aunts, uncles and grandparents. Still with me.

Author's collection of remembrance cards

Now for the religious part. Sheila was in Boston, but by phone she'd been working on getting the priest who said the Mass at the nursing home every week to come and say a funeral Mass at the cemetery chapel. He administered the last rites twice and Paul seemed to really like him. Paul was to be buried in the triple-decker funeral plot Mother bought at Gate of Heaven Cemetery for her, Dad and Paul. It was a Catholic cemetery, and although only Monica, of the nine of us left, was still Catholic, Paul still considered himself a Catholic. So we were resigned to a Catholic service.

My cell phone rang. "No luck," Sheila said. "Paul's priest is visiting family in the Caribbean. He'll be gone for two weeks. The pastor of the parish said he couldn't send anyone else. Their policy is they will say Mass at the parish church. That's it. No prayers at the funeral home. No prayers at graveside." I conveyed the news to the group.

The four of us argued back and forth about what to do. We didn't want to have to drive 45 minutes northwest to a church none of us had ever set foot in, then drive an hour south again to the cemetery to bury him. I said I was fine with skipping the whole thing. But that set off Ilene. "He would have wanted a priest," she kept saying.

The funeral director, Anthony, interrupted. He straightened his tie, stretched his neck, loosened his collar, and said, "Wait. I can help you."

We stopped and listened.

"I got a guy."

He flipped through his book of business cards and pointed to the one in question. "This guy is a chaplain for the FBI. Chaplains are authorized to do services in any faith. He can do everything except the communion thing. Is that important to you?"

We shook our heads.

It seemed fitting. Paul had spent many years working for the FBI.

His guy could do 15 minutes at the funeral home before we closed the coffin and another 5 or 10 minutes graveside. Patrick, who was a Seventh Day Adventist, wanted his pastor to do the job. But Anthony explained the New York Archdiocese was strict. Only a Catholic priest or authorized chaplain could perform the commitment ritual at the cemetery.

My eyes kept tearing up and my feet felt heavy as lead. I couldn't believe that my brother was dead. And we had to deal with turf wars.

Anthony was on the phone. He covered the mouthpiece and looked over at us. "Is 9:30 a.m. okay?" Our guy had a gig that afternoon in Queens. "He's gotta be on the road by noon." We had wanted 10 a.m., but agreed to 9:30.

We had a service of our own making at the funeral home

on Sunday evening. John and Tim, Paul's old friends from high school showed up, as well as our children, tons of friends, and a few of our cousins from Detroit and Cleveland. A case worker brought Marty. Patrick's pastor spoke. John and Patrick sang a song and played their guitars. They'd adapted a song by Styxx, "Dear Paul, we'll miss you." Patrick's wife, Shelley, sang and played hymns on the organ. Most of us got up and read something we'd written about Paul. Ilene spoke about how we all had sing-song names at home. Sheila was *Sheila Horse*, Johnny was *Flan the Man*, Paul was *Tall Paul*, as in *"Tall Paul, Tall Paul, Tall Paul, He's my all,"* sung by Annette Funicello. She made all nine of us get up and sing it together.

Our chaplain, Reverend Dave met us at the funeral home at 9:00 the next morning. We held a short cram session at the mahogany dining table in the back room, giving him the basics on Paul, his schizophrenia, his optimism, the big family, then left the guy to prepare.

Paul lay in his casket in the viewing chapel, an arrangement of plants at either end of the casket. Instead of floral arrangements, Grace, Ilene and Johnny had bought live plants so we could save them. Peace plants, New Guinea impatiens, small azalea bushes. Friends had sent flowers.

People were arriving. The relatives, a few of the friends. Everyone sitting in folding chairs in rows. Lots of sniffling.

Reverend Dave made a grand entrance wearing black robes like an Episcopalian minister or Cambridge don and led the assembled multitudes in prayer. He bounced through this psalm and that psalm, readings from the New Testament and the Old.

Eternal rest grant unto him, O Lord, and let perpetual light shine upon him. May the souls of the faithful departed through the mercy of God rest in peace.

Amen, the group answered.

The Lord is my Shepherd; I shall not want. He maketh me to

lie down in green pastures; He leadeth me beside the still waters...
Surely goodness and mercy shall follow me all the days of my life, and I
will dwell in the house of the Lord forever.

He read the eulogy my sister Monica had written and delivered the evening before and had left on a chair someplace. He read the poem about the butterfly from the back of Paul's memorial card. He read the verses to the song Patrick and John had sung the night before.

> *Dear Paul, I knew you*
> *About as well as anyone*
> *We were the wild ones*
> *So sure those days would never end*
> *Now they're only*
> *Memories, my friend*
> *Dear Paul, I'll see you*
> *Someday again.*

All of it with barely a second between acts.

I was sitting with my head bowed. What was this guy doing? This verse, that psalm. I hoped Ilene wasn't upset. She was so insistent that we have a Catholic part to the service. I looked up absentmindedly and caught the gaze of my sister, Grace. She was trying to suppress a laugh. Immediately I felt the corners of my mouth twitch up.

My eyes were red and swollen. But now they also crinkled. I let out a little *pwp pop* and sent my eyes back to the floor to compose myself.

The absurdity of it! It so fit Paul. The gibberish. What did any of it mean, anyway? I looked up again and Grace and her wife Glenda were both giggling. The chaplain's psalm salad was such a fit. Without intending it, we'd found the perfect service for Paul

"I am the resurrection and the life; whoever believes in me, even if he dies, will live, and everyone who lives and believes in me will never die," he continued.

The laugh came spitting out of my lips. Sheila, who was sitting behind me, poked me and made shushing noises. And then I saw that Ilene was cracking up, as well.

Dave sprinkled holy water on the casket from a little plastic bottle he carried in his pocket and recited lots of "Lord's" and "Almighty's" and "World without end, Amen's." More sprinkling. He stood in front of the casket and led the group in a "Hail Mary."

Now and at the hour of our death, Amen.

I knew the service meant something for many of the attendees, so I was glad we did something, but I was also glad it was over.

Sheila had propped a picture of the family into Paul's jacket pocket. What else could we have sent along with him? What could he use in the next life? A head shot of Clint Eastwood? His children's edition of *Last of the Mohicans*? False teeth?

Ilene sobbed and hung on Paul's body. "Oh, Paul." She could hardly stop.

The casket closed, Willie ushered Ilene out to their car, and the funeral procession wound its way down the Saw Mill Parkway to Gate of Heaven for the last act. Reverend Dave intoned a few more psalms. The funeral director slipped me an envelope with the deed to the cemetery plot and his bill.

And then we were all sitting around on my deck eating chicken picatta and eggplant rolitini and drinking Corona beer. The Paul memorabilia were all over the place. It was a beautiful sunny day. No Reverend Dave, no funeral director. Just us; no Paul.

After most people had gone, my husband, Ken, pulled out a wooden box labeled "PAUL" in magic marker. It had been sitting in our basement since Mother died. We set it next to the pile of Paul's things sent home from the nursing home – Paul's DVD player and collection of DVDs and CDs, a few books, a little pile of tattered and stained clothes. In the box were a bowling pin – a memento of his tenth birthday party at the local bowling alley; two football trophies from junior high school; a picture album with snapshots through about his fifth grade - several with red magic marker scribbled over Paul's hair; and a stash of letters to Paul, mostly from his two druggy friends whose parents had moved away to try to break up the bad chemistry that happened when the three of them got together. *Hey, they have some good weed up here,* one of them read. *I got really fucked up last weekend* another one said. *I keep my shit hidden in my radio.*

There were also several empty envelopes, including one from the Youth Conservation Corps addressed to Pablo Flannery, postmarked July 1975. No letter. Ilene says he had applied to work for them, had talked about it for months.

Ilene looked at the stash and said, "This was his life. 48 years and this is all he has."

We packed the memorabilia back into the box and Ilene took it home with her. The trophies went to her mantle, next to her own high school swimming trophy.

29. A different Christmas

We were all stunned. After eight months of daily emails, telephone calls and conferences with doctors and social workers, the quiet stung.

As summer blurred into autumn, we all knew that Christmas would be difficult. Ilene, in particular, dreaded facing it – her birthday – without her twin.

After Ilene graduated from high school and Paul was committed, Ilene had followed Grace out to Chicago. She met a man from the Chicago area and they eventually settled in Wisconsin. So through the 80's, when the New York area family got together at our parents' house for Christmas, there was usually only one Christmas tree cake, for Paul. He'd be brought down from the hospital upstate for the day. (Ilene, surrounded by her Illinois in-laws, got used to celebrating her birthday singly.)

By 1990 the Flannery feast had moved to my house, where the dinner menu became more varied, sometimes turkey or even lasagna instead of Mother's roast beef. Brothers, sisters, in-laws, nieces and nephews scattered over tables in the dining room, kitchen, and pretty much every available coffee table or other flat surface. But desert remained the same. And as it had been in our parents' house, dinnertime was primarily Paul's birthday, no longer Christmas. We'd buy him things he could lose or give away – new knit caps, sweatshirts, books about Native Americans, videos of Clint Eastwood or James Bond movies. "I *am* Clint Eastwood," he often said. "I think this was my best one," he said about *Hang 'em High*. And, of course, his stand out James Bond performance was *Live and Let Die*.

After dinner, we would dim the lights and gather in one room to sing the birthday song as loud and raucously as we could. My sister Charlotte, family cake maker, would also have made a batch of cupcakes for Paul to take back to the hospital and share with the other men on his ward or at his adult home.

After Ilene's twin sons graduated from high school and she and her husband moved back to the New York area, we again had two birthdays to celebrate on Christmas. Ilene was much pickier than Paul about enforcing all the rules for the day – she'd make a point of lounging around in the den while the rest got dinner on the table. Grinning like an eight-year-old, she'd announce after dinner, "I don't have to help with dishes. It's my birthday." She and Paul sat next to each other and beamed while we all sang to them over the candles on their tree-shaped cakes. Ilene also took over the job of driving Paul back to Hedgewood, the box of cupcakes and presents toted out to their car under her husband Willie's arm.

After Paul's death, Ilene had trouble focusing at work. She didn't eat, didn't shower, and eventually was suspended

217

from her job. With some prodding from all of us, she saw a doctor for the depression but became fixated on how she would spend her first Christmas without her twin. "It's supposed to be the two of us. I uprooted my family to come east and care for him, and now he's gone." Only one cake, no one beside her for the singing, no box of cupcakes to take back to Paul's home.

At Thanksgiving she announced, "I can't face it. I just want to spend the day at home with Willie and the boys."

After much persuasion, though, she relented and joined us after all, but only on the condition that no one sing happy birthday, mention her birthday, or bake her a cake.

We respected her wishes.

No one mentioned Paul, although his face looked out on us from pictures around the den. And for the first time in forty-eight years, it was Christmas all day long.

For dessert, we had pie.

***

I sleepwalked through the holidays. Afterwards, as I took down the tree ornaments and the little angel statues, untied the red velvet bows from the living room lamps and packed everything away, I felt a terrible unease, like the world as I had known it was gone.

When Mother died, I felt like this. She was the center of the family and I worried that the faraway siblings, Grace and Ilene, Sheila and Johnny, would gradually drift away. With Mother gone, would they ever come back east to visit? Now, with Paul gone, our one remaining common cause had come to an end.

I wound up his trust. As trustee, I had been charged by Mother's will to distribute any proceeds in the event of his death to the nine remaining siblings. I felt guilty accepting my share and donated some to NAMI. I wished it could have been used as Mother had hoped it would, to help maintain Paul in an apartment.

218

Ilene began to shake herself loose. Long a member of NAMI, she joined the Treatment Advocacy Center as well, and started a non-profit called Paul's Legacy Project. She began blogging about the need for community group homes for those suffering from severe mental illness and lobbying legislators to repeal the IMD exclusion.

I began to feel like myself again. I slept through the night and didn't wake up with a feeling of dread. I got back to projects I'd left half done, books I'd started, community projects I'd stuck a toe into before I'd shut down, before I'd nursed Paul. Sheila came to visit and we went in to the museums with no side trip to a mental hospital as an excuse. I secured a place on the board of directors of a little start-up bank. I could almost feel the cobwebs starting to lift.

***

That spring I attended a retreat conducted by a writing teacher at Wisdom House, a retreat house in rural Connecticut run by the Sisters of Holy Wisdom. I'd been estranged from the Catholic Church for years, even more so after that parish priest wouldn't come to deliver prayers at Paul's burial. But the retreat leader that spring wasn't Catholic. This would be a writers' retreat, a group of women dusting off our spiritual selves to find out what drove our strongest writing.

Red barns, inefficient old, white clapboard farmhouses and large, institutional brick dormitories mixed together at the center, nestled into upstate Connecticut's wooded, rolling hills. The grassy quiet of a hundred years ago. It was the beginning of May, when the tulips were hanging on to their last bits of red and yellow and old overgrown lilacs had begun their showy purple display. A week of rain let up for the weekend and a pale blue sky made a timid show. Everywhere was the fresh green of spring.

Our group had the run of the big farmhouse, used as the original convent when the sisters bought the property fifty years

219

before.   I had a tiny cell with a Spartan single bed and mismatched table, lamp and chair. I was seldom actually in the room except to sleep or write in my journal. Several times a day I joined up with the other women to write and meditate. With the great weather, I used free time to walk around the grounds.

And wherever I went, Paul's spirit insisted on joining me in my reverie. Memories of his troubled life and his lingering death haunted my thoughts. Suddenly, after not crying for months, I was in tears four or five times a day.

I went out alone at dawn to walk the grassy labyrinth, down on the lower meadow, hands held in the clasped sign of prayer, and I felt Paul hovering beside me. Later, his smile and raspy voice lurked in the shadows as our group lounged on the worn couches in the farmhouse living room. When the group talked about totems and their meaning for early people, I remembered taking Paul to the Bronx Zoo when my daughters were young, before he got too unmanageable. He kept stopping at all the totem pole displays to knock on the wood and ask in a loud voice for the spirits to come out and join us.

I chose an eagle as my totem for the weekend and remembered the day when Paul and I stood looking out over the Hudson River near the Bear Mountain Bridge, watching an eagle circle overhead and talking about reincarnation. I found myself wondering again, in this place of peace and renewal, about what awaits us after death. Paul found comfort in the belief that our parents and dog would be waiting for him when he got to heaven. I envied him his simple confidence.

I finally realized toward the end of the second day that it was the anniversary of Paul's death.

When we broke for writing time, I visited the little chapel. The stained glass in its windows didn't harbor the usual parade of fathers of the church, or even the occasional female virgin and martyr holding aloft the instruments of her own demise.   These milky, colored panels were inspired by the

Wisdom scriptures, which speak of God as Wisdom, *Sophia*, the artisan of all creation. They were impressionistic displays of angles and swirls, giving a glimpse of tall grasses in greens and golds, and splashes of light in yellows, oranges and blues. Abundant nature, thriving pastures and swirling rivers in light and clear air. As the Wisdom Scriptures say, "Against wisdom, evil does not prevail." (Wisdom 7:29-30)

Paul's spirit was near me here, in these woods and rolling hills. No more institutions. No more scalpings. No more shootings. He was free, at peace.

About the Author

Katherine Flannery Dering

Katherine Flannery Dering holds an MFA in Creative Writing from Manhattanville College. Her poetry and essays have appeared in Inkwell Magazine, as well as The Bedford Record Review, Northwoods   Press, Sensations   Magazine, Pandaloon Press, Poetry Motel and Pink Elephant Magazine. A narrative non-fiction piece, which later became a chapter of Shot in the Head, was included in Stories from the Couch, an anthology of essays about coping with mental illness.

Earlier in her career, Ms Flannery Dering earned an MA in Spanish literature from SUNY Buffalo, where she was an instructor of Spanish.   She also holds an MBA from the University of Minnesota. After a 25 year career in business, she is the retired chief financial officer of Provident Bank, a large community bank in Rockland County, New York. She now serves on the board of directors of The Westchester Bank, in Yonkers, New York.

About the Cover Art and Artist

Sandra Yuen MacKay is a visual artist and writer, residing in Vancouver, British Columbia. Despite having a mental illness, she earned a Fine Arts Diploma from Langara College and a bachelor's degree in art history from the University of British Columbia. She is also a speaker on recovery and gives talks to mental health consumers, students, families and professionals.

She exhibits her acrylic painting locally. The cover art of this book is titled "Fraternal" and is actually half of a diptych about genes being alike but different in fraternal twins, resulting in similarities and differences between them. Fraternal also refers to brotherhood, or groups or organizations with commonality. Her writing has appeared in *The Bulletin, Front Magazine, The Prairie Journal*, and other publications. She also wrote a memoir *My Schizophrenic Life: The Road to Recovery from Mental Illness*, published by Bridgeross Communications, and *Hell's Fire*, a scifi e-book.

In 2012, she received the Courage to Come Back Award in mental health in British Columbia and was chosen as a Face of Mental Illness in a national campaign. Also Sandra was awarded the Queen Elizabeth II Diamonhd Jubilee Medal for being an artist and writer, and overcoming great obstacles, to become an advocate and spokesperson on mental health issues.

Acknowledgments

I have received help and encouragement from many people on my journey from CFO to writer. Many thanks go to to Mary Carroll Moore, for years of support and wisdom. And to Emily Hanlon and Neela Vaswani, who each encouraged me to experiment. To my journal group, brave souls. To Liz Aslami and Karol Nielsen, who read my nearly final drafts of *Shot in the Head* and encouraged me to keep going. To my husband, Ken, an excellent proof reader. And thanks to my sisters Sheila, who "corrected" my memory in a few places, and Ilene, who not only helped to order the sequence of events, but has also been my biggest cheerleader. And to Marvin Ross, my publisher, who has had the patience to guide this first time author through the process.

My thanks also to The Hudson Valley Writers' Center, for providing a community for new authors. And to all the folks at the MAW and MFA programs at Manhattanville College, professors and fellow students, and especially Sister Ruth Dowd RSCJ, who wouldn't let me just take a couple of courses, but insisted I sign up for the program.